AF540863

FARM WOMEN

THEIR ROLES AND TRAINING NEEDS

FARM WOMEN
THEIR ROLES AND TRAINING NEEDS

BALA SINGH MALIK
Division of Dairy Extension
National Dairy Research Institute
Karnal (Haryana)
INDIA

DISCOVERY PUBLISHING HOUSE
NEW DELHI—110 002

Published by :

Discovery Publishing House
4831/24, Ansari Road, Prahlad Street
Darya Ganj, New Delhi—110 002 (INDIA)
Phone : 327 92 45
Fax.: 91-11-3253475

First Published—1997

Reprinted: 2013

ISBN 81-7141-391-9

Laser Typeset by :

Allied Computers,
Karnal (Haryana)

Printed at: Dynamic printers, Delhi

DEDICATED

TO MY

BELOVED PARENTS

CONTENTS

PREFACE

The women in present age are facing the most challenging situation of performing their roles in and outise the home for social and economic development of the nation. In wake of modernization of agriculture, they are playing an important role in adoption of scientific agriculture and Dairy Farming practices. There are 321 million female population in the country and majority of them are confined to rural India. This study has been conducted to know their role performance and training needs regarding improved Dairy Farming practices.

The present book deals with the role and training needs of farm women in Animal caring activities. Most of the activities relating to animals are being performed by females in rural areas in India. The training programmes; conducted by the government departments and voluntary organisations meant for male counter parts. Farm women rarely participate in training programme related to animal husbandry. When the most of the roles are being performed by farm women it is necessary to organise training programmes for women by which they can acquire knowledge and skill for getting better production from their dairy animals.

In general, the required changes in husbandry for improved livestock farming involve control of disease, improved nutrition (especially in the dry season), improved; management and breed; improvement. In arid areas the provision of water; can also be necessary as well as marketing service to encourage the sale of animals so that only the fittest animals are kept to feed in the finely-balanced ecological conditions which are vulnerable to overstocking.

Bala Singh Malik

ACKNOWLEDGEMENTS

It is my proud privilege to express my gratitude and heart-felt thanks to Dr. R.L. Kherde, Principal Scientist for his learned counsel, valuable guidance, constructive criticism and kind encouragement during the investigation and organization of this work.

Words cannot express my deep sense of gratitude to Dr. K.C. Tyagi, Head, Division of Dairy Extension and advisory committee member for his valuable suggestions, incisive guidance and constructive criticisms at various stages of my study.

My sincere thanks are due to other advisory committee members Dr. K.N.S. Sharma, Dr. Ram Chand, Head, KVK/TTC, Dr. Sukhbir Singh and Dr. T.S. Sohal for the help rendered during the research project.

I wish to record my sincere thanks to Dr. R.K. Patel, Director NDRI, Karnal for making the facilities available at every stage of my research.

I am extremely thankful to Dr. S.V.N. Rao and Mr. K.K. Saharia and Mr. P.K. Jain for their kind cooperation at various stages.

I am also thankful to Dr. Omvir Singh and Mr. J.P.S. Chauhan for their constant encouragement and needed help.

Thanks are also due to Mr. P.C. Mittal, Mr. K.N. Chaubey, Mr. B. Murali Mohan, Mr. S.P. Singh and Ch. Randhir Singh. I am also thankful to Mr. Pawan Kumar Gupta for typing this research project.

I am grateful to all of my family members for the moral support, infusing love and encouragement provided throughout the study period.

Bala Singh Malik

1
INTRODUCTION

Be it civilization development, prosperity or upliftment, prosperity or upliftment, women all over the world have been playing an interesting role since the prehistoric days. But in the present day world, women have all too often been perceived as invisible, underpaid resources with minimal influence on farm productivity and from negligible to no role in decision making. Why and how the situation is such, can not be explained so easily and without making an empirical kind of study on it. But the fact remains that, consciously or unconsciously, the male has long been targeted as the reference farmer and the recipient of much of the improved technologies developed in the agricultural and alike fields over the past few decades. Apart from few conferences both at national and international levels, some propaganda seminars and workshops and few campaigns just before some crucial national or international issues of political interest, no sincere effort has been made or fresh strategies are worked out for the correction of state of affairs prevailing today. It is inspite of the fact that women make decisions, initiate changes and play leadership roles in survival strategies of farm families (Lampe, 1988).

The archaeologists, anthropologists, social and agricultural scientists in general agree that it was woman who started cultivation of crops and domestication of animals and thereby initiated the art and science in farming. The fact that in developing countries, agriculture continues to absorb more than two third of the female work force as compared to less than ten percent in the industrialized marketing economies and less than 25 per cent of the centrally planned industrialized economies, is sufficient indication of what agricultural development has done to that section of population which initiated the production of food for the benefit of humanity and thereby engineered the way of civilization of the human race. Regarding the role of women in various sectors of agriculture, an estimate of the Food and Agriculture Organization (FAO, 1986) states that the percentage of women in agriculture labour force is 46 per cent in sub-Saharan Africa, 31 per cent in North Africa, middle East, 45 per cent in Asia and 40 per cent in Caribbean.

In the Indian context, mythology which exerts tremendous decisive force in many of the aspects of social life even today, ascribes a divine status to women in terms of "Lakashmi", "Durga" and "Saraswati" three great Goddesses of prosperity, power and wisdom, respectively. The ancient scriptures say that God lives where women are worshipped. This saying has far reaching implications to believer. But the change of value orientations, needs, attitudes, and the concept of changes in the name of attempt for modernization probably brought a radical change in the whole affair. Therefore, the post vedic period has diluted the ancient concept and philosophy regarding women and their contribution to society in particular. As a result of gradually, and consciously or unconsciously women started becoming a dependent lot. Advancements, technologies and methodologies tended to bypass them. They have been neglected in our developmental processes and gradually got isolated inspite of the fact that men and women are complementary to each other. The development of the community, society or the nation in any field irrespective of the social, economic or political factors depends on women men alike.

The Seventh Five Year Plan document of the Planning Commission states—recently a declining trend has been observed in the employment of women labourers. Some of the new technologies have displaced women from many of the traditional activities. The Green Revolution has led to increase in demand for casual labour, dispossession of small holders from their land and consequently pushing out of women from such small holdings to become wage earners. Though many of the tasks performed by males are getting mechanized, the women continue to toil in labour intensive jobs. Women get limited job opportunities in modern occupations/travels as they do not get access to the training required for new technologies. In many area where multiple crops are grown, the work load of women has increased. Again, the National Perspective Plan for Women (1988) describe the challenges ahead in the forecoming words. "Agriculture and allied fields provide employment to the largest sector of women. It largely determines socio-economic status of the rural women. In case of both agriculture, and animal husbandry and veterinary, development strategies have very insignificant role in upliftment of women in comparison to their active involvement in both the sectors." The National Commission on Self-Employed Women (1989) also observed that "Modernization and technological changes have affected women adversely. The introduction of new technology in the long run requires new skills. Women do not have access to these skills and training. Hardly any research has been done to evolve technology which will improve and alleviate their drudgery by developing tools which will make the work simple". Even the father of the nation Mahatma Gandhi argued that women's productive abilities and mental attitudes were essential forces that need to be allowed full and free play for human and social development with justice and dignity.

Inspite of realizations, proclaims and researches for upliftment of status of rural women in India the reality exists that social status of women has deteriorated and continue to do so, for the last couple of years. Crimes against them both in physical, psychological and social levels have been increasing day by day. On the other hand, the over possessive male dominates social systems all over the country, particularly in the rural areas where norms and rituals have been created for women in such a way that the gender discrimination has become an order of the day in all spheres of our lives and they are made to live in a society devoid of freedom, social injustice and unequal opportunities.

Since 1970s, a global concern for women's emancipation in all spheres has been expressed. In India, such efforts have also been made by different Ministries/Departments and Non-Government Organisations through different schemes and programmes. But in a vast country like India, the impact of such efforts has hardly been felt. In case of Agriculture where involvement of women is far more prominent, the situation is no better. In fact, the agricultural development system has not yet taken farm women population seriously in the main stream of its development processes. Realizing this fact the former Director General of ICAR Dr. N.S. Randhawa (1988) stated that "From the past experiences of developmental programmes, it is realised that for sustaining the tempo of agricultural growth in the country, farm women will have to be given more prominence in agriculture and allied vocations." Several of the farm and household operations in India more particularly in the belt of Western Uttar Pradesh, Haryana and Punjab, are exclusively carried out by women only. The role of women in agriculture varies with the socio economic status of the families, regional differences, cropping and animal husbandry patterns etc. The nutrition of the family entirely depends upon the vision, activities and abilities of the women of respective families. Saroj (1988).

Statement of the Problem

Based on the review of Indian studies, it could be seen that, the census of India estimated an All India economic participation rate of 21 per cent for women and 53 per cent for men in 1981 out of a population of about 68 crores of which Haryana has a share of about one crore consisting of about 70 lakhs male and 60 lakhs female individuals. Nearly 63 per cent of all economically active men was engaged in agriculture compared with 78 per cent of women. Almost 50 per cent of the rural female workers was classified as cultivators. The respective proportions of male rural workers have been reversed with 55 per cent reported as cultivators and only 24 per cent as agricultural labourers.

The policy approaches in India's rural development programme were (i) increased agricultural productivity and diversification of rural economy (ii) reduction of poverty, inequality and unemployment to achieve growth with social justice; (iii) promoting people's participation for stimulating growth and expanding the democratic base; and (iv) improving the quality of life. The participation of women in these programmes were partial to negligible resulting in a negligible to partial failure of every development programme launched in India. The reasons and causes of non-participation of women in development programmes have not yet been analysed. Few of them are very apparent and prominent like :

1. Needs and priorities of women are very different than men. Their needs also vary depending on a number of factors viz. education level, size of family, opportunity of employment, access to land and credit, social and economic standing in the community.

2. At present many of our development programmes and advanced innovative technologies are specifically designed and meant for men.
3. Women have less access to information about technology than men, both by virtue of their low educational status and their relative isolation from public life.
4. Legislative protection may not become effective because apart from legal and administrative lacunae they are not always adequately powerful to break through the barriers of socio-cultural norms and unequal power relations within the community.

There may be plenty of other reasons. But one more and basic one is the daily life style of our rural women. They put in their hard labour for the welfare of their families. They work like the soldiers of honey bees. Since morning their daily life style gets engaged in various activities like bringing drinking water from far off places, preparing food for household members, carrying food to fields for others working there, providing helping hand in farm activities, searching fire wood or preparing cow dung cakes for fuel, taking care of babies and old ones including ills, looking after the household domesticated animals, accumulating sufficient amount of grasses for animals and what not. They virtually do not have any time for themselves. But inspite of their hard labour neither the quality of their working life, nor their status have improved. That is probably the reason, the workshop held 1987 on affairs of rural women came to the conclusion that "The stark reality of poor rural womens' life is over burdened of labour for family maintenance. Unless this over burden is relieved, considerably, the creation of additional earning opportunities will either remain unutilized or will be met at the cost of their health or other responsibilities. Relieving women of the burden should be considered a non-variable part of the support services such as child care, supply of water, fuel, fodder etc."

How far and to what degree the planners, policy makers and administrators have realised it, it is not known, but there are five agricultural areas where women not only enjoy working but also get a tremendous sense of satisfaction. One such area is dairying.

India with an annual milk production of 641 lac tones in 1987-88 ranks third in the world. To increase the milk production the Govt.

has fixed the target of 65 million tones of milk production by 2000 AD. Milk and milk products being the second largest contributor to the gross agricultural produce, play a vital role in the country's agricultural economy. In India the value of milk and its products exceeded Rs. 1,00,000 million in 1984-85 ranking after rice but before wheat. Hence, milk can be regarded as India's second most important agricultural commodity, providing income to the 75% of the total population especially rural farmers. Milk provides both nutrition and supplementary income to these weaker sections. Dairy Development programmes fit in most appropriately in the country's programme of increasing production, rural employment and social justice. Thus, the contribution of dairy to the Nation's health and economic welfare is rather unique. Only a few studies were conducted with regard to the women tasks and hardly there is any study about the role of farm women in Dairy Farming Practices. It is, in this context that a study entitled "Role Performance and Training Needs of Farm Women in relation to Dairy Farming Practices in Haryana State" is proposed with the following specific objectives :

1. To identify the roles of farm women and to assess their role performance in Dairy Farming Practices.
2. To study the differential level of knowledge of farm women regarding breeding, feeding, management and health care.
3. To study the perceived training needs of farm women regarding Dairy Farming Practices.
4. To study the relationship of socio-personal, psychological variables with role performance and perceived training needs in relation to Dairy Farming Practices.

Significance of the Study

This study would help in planning and organizing training programmes in dairy farming for rural ladies by determining their felt needs. It may also give an idea that in which sub-area of Dairy Farming the training component has to be stressed. This would help the trainers in developing a sound syllabus for training programme. Further more, it would help them in deciding priority of subject matter area and sub-areas in dissemination of dairy innovations. An identification of training needs on the basis of knowledge and perception of needs would help the organizers to design the suitable training programme for rural ladies which may lead to an effective transfer of Dairy Farming Technology and thus, would help in increasing milk production and income generation.

Limitations of the Study

1. The present study was confined only to districts of Haryana state due to resource constraints of a single student researcher.
2. Only 200 farm women have been interviewed and most of the findings of the study are based on expressed opinions by them which not be completely free from their individual biases and prejudices.
3. The training needs have been worked out only for farm women regarding Dairy Farming Practices.
4. This study is restricted only to those ladies who had the milch animals and devote time for caring the animals.

Inspite of the above facts sincere attempt has been made in making the study as deep and as objective and systematic as possible.

Format of the Thesis

In addition to this introductory chapter, four more chapters have been organized. The second chapter is devoted for the review of literature. Chapter third deals with the methodology including the locale of the study. The findings and discussion are presented in chapter fourth. The last chapter deals with summary. The major findings are also given in this chapter. The implications and suggestion for present study have been included in Summary chapter.

2
REVIEW OF LITERATURE

The task of searching the literature in a scientific investigation is necessary with a view to study the technique adopted and results obtained by the earlier researchers. This provides a clue to the researcher in designing the study. A good deal of work have been done regarding training of framers and role performance of in-service persons, but very little work has been carried out on farm women's training needs in the field of Dairy Farming and their role performance.

Keeping in view the objectives and variables under study, the review of literature has been presented under the following sections:

1. Personal Variables
2. Communication Variables
3. Psychological Variables
4. Dependent Variables

Personal Variables

Age

Many of the researchers observed that the women respondents in their study were of young age ranging from 20 to 35 years. It was also revealed that age has no significant relationship with role performance and training needs of rural women (Jaswant Kaur, 1981; Om Parkash, 1988; Saroj, 1988 and Kadian, 1988). Gill and Minhas (1978) and Pawar (1979) in their studies observed that the age of the respondents was negatively and significantly associated with the perceived training needs regarding dairy farming practices.

Education

Omprakash (1988), Kadian (1988), Saroj (1988), Jaswant Kaur (1981) and Khajan Singh (1982) reported that woman respondents under their studies were illiterates to the extent of 52% to 80%

Jaswant Kaur (1981) observed that education of the farm women had no significant relationship with role performance regarding dairy farming practices whereas Omprakash (1988) found negative and significant relationship between education of farm women and perceived training needs in dairy farming practices.

Gill and Minhas (1978) concluded that education was significantly associated with training needs in all the areas of dairy farming practices. Further they observed that lesser educated respondents had comparatively higher training needs.

Pawar (1979) reported that education of farmers had positive relationship with perceived training needs in all areas of dairy farming.

Fulzele (1986) observed that education had no relationship with training needs of the farmers regarding dairy farming.

Family Education Status

Omprakash (1988) revealed in his study that 68 per cent ladies had medium family education status. Further, he observed that family education status has significant and negative relationship with perceived training needs in respect of dairy farming.

Herd Size

Saroj (1988) and Omprakash (1988) have observed that mostly farm ladies have medium herd size. Kadian (1988) reported that 61 per cent ladies have large herd size. Jaswant Kaur (1981) observed that 84 per cent rural ladies have small and medium herd size.

Omprakash (1988) reported that herd size had significant and negative relationship with the perceived training needs of farm women regarding dairy farming practices.

Jaswant Kaur (1981) observed that herd size had significant and negative relationship with role performance of farm ladies in the area of dairy farming.

Gill and Minhas (1978) observed that herd size was significantly associated with training needs of dairy farmers in all areas except breeding. They explained, the respondents owing large herds had comparatively lower training needs than the ones with small herds whereas Pawar (1979) stated that herd size had no relationship with training needs. Fulzele (1986) reported that there was significant and positive relationship between herd size and training needs regarding dairy farming.

Land Holding Size

Gill and Minhas (1978) reported that the association between size of land holding in the all areas of dairy farming except feeding was not significant. In this area large farm holders had low training needs as compared with farmers will small/marginal and medium size holdings.

Pawar (1979) observed that land holding size had no relationship with training needs whereas Omprakash (1988) found significant and negative relationship between land holding size and perceived training needs of farm women.

Fulzele (1986) reported that land holding size had positive and significant relationship with training needs.

Jaswant Kaur (1981) found that land holding size and role performance of farm women regarding dairy farming was significantly and negatively associated.

Milk Production and Disposal

Omprakash (1988) observed medium milk production level in about 65% of the households studied. He further revealed that milk production and consumption had significant and negative relationship with the perceived training needs of farm women regarding dairy farming practices.

Directorate of Animal Husbandry, Gujarat (1971) in its sample survey report pointed out that 26.00 per cent of the farmers produced 5.00 litres or more quantity of milk while 22.00 per cent of the producer's household produced one litre or less quantity of milk.

Family Size

Jaswant Kaur (1981) and Khajan Singh (1982) reported that majority of the farm women had medium family size while Saroj (1988) observed that majority of female household had large family size. Jaswant Kaur (1981) also observed the family size had no relationship with role performance of farm ladies.

Caste

Jaswant Kaur (1981) and Khajan Singh (1982) have observed that 90.00 per cent farm ladies belonged to the higher caste whereas, Saroj (1988) and Omprakash (1988) reported that 80.00 per cent farm women belonged to middle caste groups. Jaswant Kaur (1981) revealed that caste was significantly and positively related with the role performance of farm women in respect of dairy farming practices.

Omprakash (1988) observed that caste had significant but negative correlation with perceived training needs of rural ladies in all the areas of dairy farming.

Time Spent on Dairying

Saroj (1988) reported that the time use pattern of respondents in animal care activities was significantly different when seasons as well as various land holding 1 hr. 26 minutes were spent in peak and 2 hrs. 37 minutes during slack seasons on these activities. Where land holdings were considered, the time spent varied from 1 hr. 38 minutes (Marginal) to 2 hrs. 39 minutes (Medium). All the women from medium and large holdings were involved in animal related activities irrespective of season. Infact, more than 70.80 per cent involvement of rural women was observed in animal related activities.

Omprakash (1988) observed that farm women devote about 21.96, 19.38, 18.33 and 5.33 per cent time in home management, dairying, agriculture and miscellaneous activities respectively.

Chakravorty (1975) conducted a study in some villages of Rohtak district and revealed that an active farm women spends 8 to 9 hrs. on the farm during the peak agricultural season, 3 to 4 hrs. on taking care of the animals and 3 to 4 hrs. on household work.

Verma and Malik (1984) found that rural women in India still pay more attention to their domestic work wherein, on an average, they spent 5 hrs. 3 min. per day. It was followed by animal husbandry. It was found that a considerable amount of time equal to 3 hrs. 15 minutes daily was devoted to care of dairy animals by the rural women.

Gupta & Singh (1986) observed that in addition to crop raising operations, a women devoted about 11 hrs. a day on domestic and animal rearing activities.

All India Coördinated Research Project in home science at Haryana Agricultural University, Hissar (1985) studied the time disposition pattern of rural women in three district of state and revealed that on an average a rural women spent 15 hrs. 46 minutes per day in various domestic activities including animal care.

Communication Variables

Extension Contact

Kadian (1988), Saroj (1988) and Pawar (1979) observed that most of the respondents had low extension contact. Kadian (1988) observed that 91 per cent farm ladies had low and medium contacts with extension personnels. Omprakash (1988) observed that 54 per cent farm ladies had medium extension contact. He further revealed that the extension contact had significant and negative relationship with perceived training needs of farm women in the field of dairy farming.

Pawar (1979) and Fulzele (1986) reported that extension contact had no relationship with perceived training needs of farmers regarding dairy farming.

Jaswant Kaur (1981) revealed that extension contact had no relationship with role performance of farm ladies in animal related activities.

Mass Media Exposure

Jaswant Kaur (1981), Saroj (1988), Kadian (1988) and Khajan Singh (1982) reported in their studied that farm women had low mass media exposure. Omprakash (1988) revealed that 54.00 per cent of farm women had medium level of mass media exposure. Further he stated that mass media had significant and negative relationship with perceived training needs of ladies regarding animal care activities.

Pawar (1979) and Fulzele (1986) have reported that mass media exposure had no relationship with perceived training needs of dairy farmers.

Jaswant Kaur (1981) observed that mass media exposure had no relationship with role performance of rural ladies regarding dairy farming activities.

Psychological Variables

Attitude Towards Dairy Farming

Kadian (1988) reported that farm women had 21.00 per cent low, 48.00 per cent medium and 31.00 per cent high attitude towards dairy farming. Omprakash (1988) observed that farm women had unfavourable attitude towards dairy farming. He also observed that attitude towards dairy farming had significant and negative relationship with perceived training needs of farm women. Same findings have been reported by Fulzele regarding farmers.

Pawar (1979) observed that 69.00 per cent farmers had unfavourable attitude towards dairy farming. He further stated that there was significant and positive relationship with perceived training needs of farmers in the field of dairy farming.

Economic Motivation

Saroj (1988) reported that farm women had high level of economic motivation whereas Kadian (1988) and Omprakash (1988) that mostly farm women had medium level of economic motivation. Fulzele (1986) revealed that 69% farmers had high level of economic motivation. He further stated economic motivation had significant and positive relationship with training need of dairy farmers.

Omprakash (1988) had different views. He reported that economic motivation had negative association with perceived training needs of farm women regarding dairy farming practices.

Level of Aspiration

Khajan Singh (1982) concluded that majority of farm women were medium aspirant, ten areas of aspiration first, second and tenth rank were earned by milch animals education of son and material possession respectively. He further revealed that majority of rural women were having agriculture as their main occupation and dairying as subsidiary occupation and were medium aspirations.

Value Orientation (Conservatism & Progressivism)

Jaswant Kaur (1981) reported that 52.00 per cent farm women had low value orientation and 48% had high value orientation. She further observed that value orientation had no relationship with role performance of farm women regarding dairy farming.

Knowledge

Jaswant Kaur (1981) observed that farm women had low level of knowledge regarding dairy farming practices. She found that 64 per cent rural ladies possess medium level and 36 per cent had low level, none of them had high level of knowledge in dairy farming.

Kadian (1988) stated that knowledge level of farm women in relation to dairy farming was 22 per cent, 49 per cent and 29 per cent low, medium and high respectively. He further observed that the level of knowledge of farm women in the field of dairy farming had significant and negative relationship with age, whereas, education, land holding size, herd size, extension contacts and mass media exposure were positively correlated.

Omprakash (1988) observed that mostly farm women (60%) had medium level of knowledge about dairy farming. He also observed that knowledge had significant and negative relationship with perceived training needs of farm women in dairy farming.

Dependent Variables

Role Performance

Haque (1968) found that 78.66 per cent of the rural school going girls worked on farm, 79.66 per cent of them cut fodder in the fields, brought it to the farms and also chaffed it, 53.33 per cent of the girls did milking of the buffaloes and 57.33 per cent participated in feeding of cattle.

Singh (1968) studied that participation of rural women in agricultural operations in Jabalpur, and revealed that comparatively large proportions of women participated in seed storage, winnowing, harvesting and care of animals. It was observed that women belonging to the middle age group, having frequent urban contacts and formal education, coming from lower castes and possessing small land holding participated in agricultural operations in a larger proportion than others.

Puri (1974) studied the role of farm women in Najafgarh block of Delhi. The study showed that animal related tasks like bringing fodder from the field, chaffing, preparation of feed for cattle, watering, cleaning and bathing cattle, milking, making cow dung cakes, heating milk, making curd were predominantly done by women.

Singh (1979) conducted a study among the milk maids of Kaira district for studying the impact of Amul Pattern Coop. on women. She found that traditionally dairy production and milling were carried out by women particularly of the lower castes. The training courses for the care of new breeds of cattle include no single woman.

Sharma *et al* (1980) in their report studied that labour utilization pattern of different categories of labourers found that diary being the subsidiary occupation, the input of labour was mainly by family members. They found that works such as cleaning, feeding and milking of animals were attended by women and grazing of animals by children. The major portion of the female labour input was used for bringing fodder from the fields (40%) followed by feeding of animals (28%).

Jain (1980) reported that a traditional dimension of labour exists within households with respect to dairying chores. Women were generally associated with animal husbandry activities which were performed at home, for example, cattle feeding, milling, fodder preparation, shed cleaning etc. while the men generally engaged in tasks which were performed outside the home, for example, the procurement and collection of cattle feed, pasture grazing etc.

Jately (1981) analyzed the impact of planned social change and modernization in women in a study of the most developed village of one of the progressive district of Western U.P. She observed that women were increasingly participating in modern agriculture for reducing costs. Increasing wealth led to an expansion in livestock since women were responsible for caring of cattle, this leads to an increase in their work load.

Jaswant Kaur (1981) concluded in her study that 62% ladies were illiterate. She also found that female performed more number of activities than the males. Only 4% milk producers performed more number of dairy activities.

Usha Rani (1982) revealed that the women participation rate in dairy enterprise was as high as 65% as against 31 and 4% for men and children respectively. It was observed that the average work burden on a female was nearly 2964 hrs. in a year and the domestic work recorded the highest female labour used followed by dairying, accounting for about 47% and 29% of the total work days, respectively. It was observed that family labour income in dairy enterprise varied between Rs. 841/- for landless labour households and Rs. 1146/- for small farmers. Thus it may be concluded that dairying particularly with high yielding milch animals could generate additional employment and income opportunities to the households of weaker section.

Devi *et al* (1984) studied the role expectations and role performance of farm women in Krishna district of Andhra Pradesh. As regards expected roles of the rural women, harvest and post harvest role emerged as the first rank followed by pre-sowing and sowing, allied agriculture and inter-cultivation. Women belonging to small farm holdings, lower castes with low socio-economic status, less education and less urban contact were participating more in agricultural activities.

Satnam Kaur (1986) revealed that participation of women in Animal Husbandry related tasks, the 57.6 per cent of the households females alone were doing all these tasks without any help from servant or husband. In 9.27 per cent households, they shared this work with both servant and male members of the family. Thus 91.06 per cent household females participated in tasks related to animal husbandry. Highest amount of time was spent in preparing and giving feeds followed by carrying fodder, making cow dung cakes and chaffing of the fodder.

Training Needs

Kumar and Mage (1974) in their study on farm women observed the differential stress on training need areas and reported that nutrition and child care were considered more important than the agriculture areas by the farm women. The other areas preferred by them were keeping livestock, feeding animals, grain storage and care of animals.

Sharma (1974) concluded that information needs of farm women were perceived high in order of importance in respect of plant protection, seed selection, treatment, grading storage and marketing of food grains, fertilizer use, improved agriculture tools etc.

Minhas (1976) conducted a study and found that training of dairy farmers in the area of breeding, feeding, housing and animals health were high and medium in the area of management and marketing of milk.

Pawar (1979) concluded that milk producers perceived training needs in area of animal health care, breeding, management and fodder production were in descending order.

Gite (1980) suggested that in all the areas of dairy farming, breeding, feeding, management and health care, perceived training needs of respondents were high.

Kokate (1980) found that there was no significant relationship between knowledge and perceived training needs in case of wheat cultivation. Omprakash (1988) observed that about 63.30, 22.50 and 14.20 per cent farm women had perceived training needs to medium, low, and high levels respectively.

Saroj (1988) observed the areas which were preferred by rural women for training. She revealed that cloth stitching was the most preferred area (74.50%) followed by papad warian (73%) and dairy farming (71.50%).

Duration of Training

Gill (1970) concluded that the farmers training programme should be of seven to eight days duration.

Dubey *et al* (1978) observed that the women's training programme should be conducted for 3–6 days duration.

Pawar (1979) suggested that the training programme for milk producers could be organized for 3–5 days duration.

Singh *et al* (1979) reported that the dairy farmers opined that training should be of short duration for a week.

Fulzele (1986) observed that majority of the respondents (62%) preferred two days training duration.

Omprakash (1988) observed that majority of the farm women (55%) indicated that the training programme should be for 1–3 days duration.

Saroj (1988) found that farm women having large and small land holding preferred 7 days period for training while marginal and landless farm women want that training period should be two weeks duration.

Time of Training

Patil and Kale (1972) found that the suitable time for training farmers was from the month of December to May of the calender year.

Pawar (1979) viewed that the training programme for the dairy farmers could be organized in the month of March or May.

Fulzele (1986) found that the small and marginal farmers preferred best time for training programme during the off season.

Gite (1980) suggested that majority of landless crossbred cattle owners preferred time of training programme in the month of January, February and March.

Saroj (1988) stated that January, February, June and December are the most suitable months for organizing the training programme which are related to farm women.

Place of Training

Singh *et al* (1979) stated that the training programme should be arranged right in the village as opined by the dairy farmers under study.

Gite (1980) suggested that training must go to the landless crossbred cattle owners in their own village.

Omprakash (1988) and Saroj (1988) revealed that about 55 per cent farm women prefer their own village as the place of training programme.

3

RESEARCH METHODOLOGY

The term methodology refers to the process, principles and procedures by which we approach problems and seek answers. In the social sciences, this term applies to hold one conducts the research. Therefore, this chapter has been devoted to describe the methods and techniques used in conducting the study. The presentation is organised under following sub-heads :

1. Locale of Research
2. Selection of the Respondents
3. Variables and their Measurement
4. Data Collection
5. Statistical Analysis.

Locale of Research

Selection of the State

The study has been conducted in Haryana state which comprised of 12 districts. According to 1981 census the total population of Haryana was 12.92 millions and out of which 6.01 millions were females. About 78.40 per cent females belong to rural area who were engaged mostly in agriculture and dairying. They are playing important role in rural upliftment of the state inspite of their illiteracy. The Haryana state has been selected for the following reasons :

i) the progressiveness of agriculture in the state and prominent role played by women in crop and dairy farming operations;

ii) the familiarity of the researcher with the study area and ability to speak local language which are essential for eliciting proper responses.

Selection of the Districts

The districts of the state have been categorised into progressive and less progressive districts on the basis of the following 12 indicators as suggested by the experts/scientists and field workers :

Indicators

1. Literacy percentage of rural women.
2. Cattle and buffalo ratio.
3. Number of milch cows/1000 persons.
4. Number of milch buffaloes/1000 persons.
5. Density of cattle/sq. km.
6. Density of buffaloes/sq. km.
7. Percentage of crossbred cattle.
8. Per capita availability of milk in gms./day.
9. Average livestock population per veterinary institution.
10. Percentage of irrigated area.
11. Average yield of wheat and
12. Average yield of paddy.

On the basis of literacy percentage the districts were arranged in descending order from highest to lowest percentage for the district having highest percentage, a score of 12 was assigned. For the next highest district a score of 11 was assigned. Similarly a score of '1' was given to the district having lowest literacy percentage of rural women. Likewise all the districts were given scores on the basis of their respective positions on all the 12 indicators. Thus each district has got 12 scores which were later added to get the aggregate score of progressiveness. The mean was calculated which formed the basis for categorising the districts as progressive and less progressive districts. The scores ranged from 49 to 117 and the mean was 83.25. The progressive districts having scores above the mean were Kurukshetra, Sonepat, Karnal, Ambala and Jind in the descending order and the less progressive districts having scores less than mean were Hissar, Sirsa, Rohtak, Gurgaon, Bhiwani, Faridabad and Mohendergarh. Kurukshetra, the most progressive district and Mahendergarh, the least progressive district were selected for the present study. Some features of Mahendergarh and Kurukshetra districts have been described as under :

Mahendergarh District

The district is situated in the Southern most part of the state surrounded by the state of Rajasthan in its east, South and Western borders and by the districts of Gurgaon, Rohtak and Bhiwani in the Northern border from East to West. It covers an area of 3010 sq. km. out of which about 264,000 hactares of land are cultivable. The nature of the soil is sandy. Among the major crops wheat, barley, bajra, jowar, guar and oats are most common. Out of the total population of 9594000 as high as 834025 live in rural areas while only 125375 are urbanites. In the context of sex differences 496903 are male and 462497 are female. The average rainfall in the district per year is about 39.3 cm. The different places of the district are well connected with road and rail network.

Kurukshetra District

The district is situated in the Northern part of the state covering an area of about 3740 sq. km. The district boundry in the North is surrounded by the state of Punjab and Ambala district of Haryana. In the far East, the state of Uttar Pradesh and in the down South to West the districts of Karnal and Jind are situated. Out of the total area, about 334,000 hactares of land are under cultivation and the major crops sown are wheat, paddy, barseem, oats, jowar and maize. The nature of the soil is usually loam to clay loam. The total population of the district is 1130026 out of which as high as 943974 live in rural areas and 186052 are urbanites. The male and female populations are 606571 and 523445 respectively. The average rainfall in the district per year is about 52.9 cm. The district is well known for its historical importance since Mahabharata and is well connected with rail and road communications.

Selection of the Respondents

Selection of the Blocks/Villages

There were eight Development Blocks in Kurukshetra and nine in Mahendergarh district. Four blocks, Ateli and Mahendergarh from Mahendergarh district and Ladwa and Sahabad from Kurukshetra district were selected randomly from each district. The villages were selected randomly on the basis of distance from block headquarters. Two villages, one situated at distance of more than 8 kms., and another village located within 8 kms. radius from block headquarter were selected randomly from each block. Thus there were eight villages drawn from four blocks and two districts (Table 3.1 and 3.2).

SAMPLING PLAN

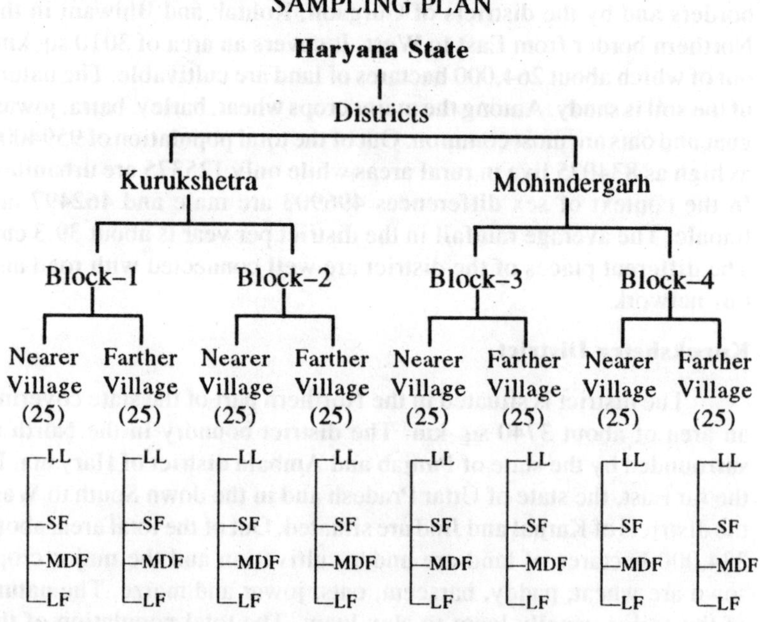

25 From each Village Among 4 Categories Proportionately
Total 200 Respondents

Selection of the Respondents

The farm women who own at least one milch cattle or buffalo and devoting time for caring the animals in Kurukshetra and Mahendergarh districts constitute the population of the study. The farm women were categorized into four categories landless, small, medium and large depending upon their land size. From the list in each village, 25 women were selected on the basis of proportionate random sampling subject to the condition of having a minimum of five respondents in each of the categories. Thus, the study comprises of 200 respondents drawn from 8 villages selected from four blocks and two districts. The list of the selected villages with the number of respondents drawn from each village is given in Table 3.1 and 3.2.

Table 3.1 : List of Sample Villages Selected and Number of Respondents

MAHENDERGARH DISTRICT				
Blocks	*Village*	*Land Holding Categories*	*Total Farm Women*	*Sample Farm Women*
Ateli	Faizepur	Landless	28	5
		Small	160	10
		Medium	40	5
		Large	18	5
	Bihali	Landless	90	6
		Small	105	7
		Medium	105	7
		Large	50	5
Mahender-garh	Jarepur	Landless	128	8
		Small	96	6
		Medium	96	6
		Large	80	5
	Khudana	Landless	198	9
		Small	132	6
		Medium	110	5
		Large	110	5

Landless	28
Small	29
Medium	23
Large	20
	100

Table 3.2 : List of Sample Villages Selected and Number of Respondents

KURUKSHETRA DISTRICT				
Blocks	***Village***	***Land Holding Categories***	***Total Farm Women***	***Sample Farm Women***
Ladwa	Badonda	Landless	120	9
		Small	65	5
		Medium	75	6
		large	65	5
	Karami	Landless	60	8
		Small	47	7
		Medium	38	5
		Large	28	5
Sahabad	Landhi	Landless	140	8
		Small	60	5
		Medium	130	7
		Large	30	5
	Dahu Majra	Landless	120	9
		Small	75	5
		Medium	105	6
		Large	20	5

Landless	34
Small	22
Medium	24
Large	20
	100

Variables and their Measurement

After consulting the relevant literature, certain important variables were selected for the study keeping in view the resources and time available with the researcher. The description of variables included in this study, their operationalization and methods followed for the measurement of each of the variable is presented in this section. As a preview, the list of variables alongwith the instrument used for their measurement is given on page 25.

Sl. No.	Variables	Measurement
INDEPENDENT VARIABLES		
1. Socio-Personal Variables		
1.	Age	Chronological age in years
2.	Respondent's Education	Schedule developed
3.	Family Education Status	Index developed
4.	Herd Size	No. of cattle & buffaloes
5.	Land Holding Size	Area under operation in acres
6.	Milk production and disposal	Total milk production, consumption and sale in litres/day
7.	Family Size	No. of family members
8.	Caste	Scale developed by Trivedi (1963)
9.	Time spent on dairying activities	Scheduled developed
2. Communication Variables		
1.	Extension Contact	Index developed by Chauhan (1976)
2.	Mass Media Exposure	Index developed by Chauhan (1976)
3. Psychological Variables		
1.	Attitude towards dairy farming	Scale developed by Gupta (1976)
2.	Economic motivation	Scale developed by Gupta (1976)
3.	Level of aspiration	Scale developed by Ram Chand (1983)
4.	Value orientation (Conser-(vatism–progressivism)	Scale developed by Mulary & Roy (1973)
5.	Knowledge	Test developed
DEPENDENT VARIABLES		
1.	Role Performance	Schedule developed
2.	Perceived training needs	Schedule developed

DESCRIPTION OF THE VARIABLES

Socio-Personal Variables

1. Age

It refers to chronological age of the respondents rounded to nearest whole number at the time of investigation and was ascertained by direct questioning. Each year was given one score.

2. Respondent's Education

It refers to the level of education attained by the respondent. This means the ability to read and write in accordance with the formal education received by way of the number of years spent in schools and colleges and standard passed. This was measured with the help of schedule. The scoring was given as below :

Category	Score
Illiterate	0
Can read	1
Can read & write	2
Primary School	3
Middle School	4
High School	5
Graduation & above	6

3. Family Education Status

It refers to education of all family members above 6 years of age eligible for formal education and was ascertained through direct questioning. The scores were assigned as mentioned above.

$$\text{Family Education Status} = \frac{\text{Total number of education score of all eligible family members}}{\text{No. of eligible family members}}$$

4. Herd Size

It refers to the number of cattle and buffalo heads owned by the respondents and the same was measured by directly questioning the respondent.

5. Land Holding Size

It refers to the number of acres of land under operation of the respondent irrespective of ownership status and was measured by directly questioning the respondent. One score to every acre of farm area was assigned for the purpose of analysis.

6. Milk Production and Disposal

It refers to the quantity of milk produced in litre by the herd of respondents on previous day of the interview. Milk disposal refers to as the total quantity of milk sold and consumed by the respondents/ households in litres on the day prior to investigation.

7. Family Size

Family size refers to the number of persons living under one roof and eating the food from the same kitchen. It was measured through a direct question. A unit score of '1' was given to each member of the family of the respondent.

8. Caste

It refers to one's belonging to distinct social class on hereditary lines. The socio-economic status scale developed by Trivedi (1963) was used to quantify this variable.

9. Time Spent on Dairy Farming Activities

It has been operationalized as the total hours spent by the respondent to perform different dairy farming activities in day. Initially a list of 23 possible activities regarding dairy farming was prepared based on literature, experts opinion and personal experience. These are the possible activities on which rural women devote their time in dairy farming. The respondents were asked to indicate the amount of time they spent on each of these activities. The time was indicated in hours per day.

Communication Variables

1. Extension Contact

The number of visits made by an individual respondent to

extension agents viz. Livestock Assistant, Veterinary Surgeon, Gram Sewak, Agriculture Development Officer, Block Development Officer, Bank Personnel and Progressive farmers and vice versa was construed as extension contact. It has been measured through the index developed by Chauhan (1976).

2. *Mass Media Exposure*

It refers to the degree of utilization or exposure to mass media of communication viz. radio, television, newspaper and farm magazines. The index developed by Cahuhan (1976) was used to quantify mass media exposure of the respondents.

Psychological Variables

1. *Attitude towards Dairy Farming*

Attitude is generally defined as the tendency to respond either favourably or unfavourably towards certain persons, objects, situations or ideas (Krech and Crutch Field, 1948). According to Thurstone (1946) attitude is the degree of positive and negative effects associated with some psychological object. In this study, attitude means the tendency of the individual to respond favourably or unfavourably towards dairy farming. The attitude of the respondents was ascertained by adopting the scale of Gupta (1976). The score 3, 2 & 1 was assigned to the positive statement and vice versa in case of negative statement respectively as given below :

Agree = 3

Undecided = 2

Disagree = 1

2. *Level of Aspiration*

Aspiration may be defined as "The level of future performance in a familiar task which an individual with his level of past performance in that task explicity undertake to reach" (Frank, 1935). Level of aspiration has been operationalized for this study as the respondent's goals like occupation, income, education, herd size, milk production and so on as a consequence of the transfer of dairy farming technology through training. This was measured by using the scale developed by Ram Chand (1983).

3. Economic Motivation

Economic motivation may be defined as "The process of arousing action, sustaining the activity in progress and regulating the pattern of activity" (Cofer and Appley, 1964). In this present study economic motivation refers to the occupation in terms of profit maximization and the relative value placed by dairy farm women on economic ends. The economic motivation of the respondent was measured by the scale developed by Gupta (1976).

4. Value Orientation (Conservatism–progressivism)

Conservatism is a positive attitude of the individual towards precedence and maintenance of status-quo and hence unfavourable to the adoption of new ideas. Likewise, progressivism is a positive attitude of the individual to change and to the adoption of new ideas.

The value orientation (Conservatism and progressivism) scale developed by Mulay and Ray (1973) was adopted to measure this variable. The scale consisted of eight statements arranged on a four point continuum ranging from strongly agree to strongly disagree. Barring items nos. 4 and 7, the rest were negative statements. For positive items 4, 3, 2 and 1 scores were assigned for strongly agree, agree, disagree and strongly disagree responses respectively whereas the pattern of scoring was reversed for negative items. The theoretical score ranged from 8 to 32.

5. Knowledge Regarding Improved Dairy Farming Practices

Knowledge is generally understood as an intimate acquaintance of an individual with facts. Bloom et al (1956) considered knowledge as those behaviours and test situations which emphasise remembering either by recognition or recall of ideas, material or phenomena. English and English (1958) defined knowledge as "the body of understood information possessed by an individual or by a culture". They further explained knowledge as that part of a person's information which is in accord with established facts. Rogers and Shoemaker (1971) described knowledge as a function or a stage of the decision process when the "individual is exposed to an innovation's existence and gain some understanding of how it functions." Singh and Singh (1976) stated that knowledge is the totality of understood informatioin possessed by a person. In the present study knowledge refers to the understanding of the farm women about improved dairy farming practices.

A suitable knowledge test was developed and standardized for this study as per the guidelines of Lindquist (1951). The steps followed in developing the knowledge test for this study are :

1. Collection of items
2. Formulation of questions
3. Item analysis
   — Difficulty Index
   — Discrimination Index
   — Point-biserial correlation
4. Reliability
5. Validity

1. Collection of items

The content of the knowledge test is composed of items. A list of items on package of practices for dairy farming practices applicable to the study area was prepared by consulting extension literature, the scientists of NDRI, Karnal and veterinary personnel working in the State Department of Animal Husbandry.

Forty six items pre-presenting the improved dairy farming practices covering breeding, feeding, management, health care and clean milk production were collected.

2. Formulation Questions

Questions of objective nature were formulated on the basis of the 46 items. These questions were so developed keeping in view that they

a) should promote thinking

b) should have certain difficulty value

c) should differentiate the well informed from the less knowledgeable.

3. Item Analysis

The initially prefaced 46 items were administered to 30 non

sample respondents of the study area. Their responses were then quantified by assigning '1' to the correct answer and 'O' to wrong answer or no response for dichotomous questions. For multiple choice questions the scores assigned were 3, 2 and 1 to most accurate, accurate and least accurate responses. A respodent's total score was obtained by summation of his score on all the questions. These scores were utilized for calculating difficulty index, discrimination index and point bi-serial correlation.

i) *Difficulty Index* : Index of item difficulty is the percentage of respondents answering an item correctly. The difficulty of an item varies from individual to individual. When a respondent answers an item correctly, it was assumed that the item was less difficult than his ability to cope with it. The assumption was that, the item difficulty was lineraly related to the level of respondent's knowledge about dairy farming practices. The difficulty index for each of the 46 items was calculated by dividing the total correct responses for a particular item by total number of responses as under :

D. I. = NC/n

where,

D.I. = Difficulty Index

NC = Number of respondents answering an item correctly.

n = Total number of respondents

The difficulty indices of these items range from 25 to 75.

ii) *Discrimination Index* : If a statement is answered by some respondents correctly and not by others, such a statement has greater power to discriminate more knowledgeable from the less knowledgeable persons than another statement which is either answered correctly by every one or none in the sample. If a statement is so simple than it is correctly answerable by every one, it does not have the power to discriminate the respondents with varying levels of knowledge. In a way, the items having higher discrimination power implicitly indicate that such items are moderately difficult, and they discriminate the respondents who answer it correctly from those who are unable to do so. The discrimination power of all the 46 raw items were worked out with the help of low and high criterion groups.

Initially the respondents were arranged in descending order on the basis of their total score obtained in the knowledge test. Out of this list, top 25 per cent and bottom 25 per cent of the respondents were demarcated and considered as high and low groups. For each question the numbe of top 25 per cent (NH) and bottom 25 per cent (NL) who answered it correctly were counted.

The discrimination index was calcuated adopting the formula :

$$DI = \frac{NH-NL}{n}$$

where,

DI = Discrimination index

NH = Number of respondents in 25 per cen high group who answered correctly.

NL = Number of respondents in 25 per cent low group who answered correctly.

n = Number of respondents in 25 per cent sample

iii) *Point Biserial Correlation* : The point biserial correlation was calculated for all the 46 items, by using the procedure described by Garrett (1966). It was calculated to know the internal consistency of the item. The point biserial correlation was calculated by the following formula :

$$r_{pbis} = \frac{\overline{x} - \overline{x}q}{6} \times \sqrt{pq}$$

where,

r_{pbis} = Point biserial correlation coefficient

$\overline{x}p$ = Mean score of those answering the item correctly.

$\overline{x}q$ = Mean sore of those answering the item incorrectly. Standard deviation of the entire sample

p = Proportion of the sample answering the items correctly.

q = 1–p

All the items having difficulty indices between 0.25 to 0.75, discrimination index above 20 and r_{pbis} significant at 5 per cent level were finally selected for the final knowledge test which contained 20 items.

4. Reliability

The reliability of the knowledge test was assessed by test retest method. The instrument composing 20 items was administered twice, at an interval of 15 days to 25 randomly selected respondents of a village other than the selected village in the study area. The items were scored separately for both the tests and correlation coefficient was worked out. The correlation coefficient obtained (0.782) was found significant at 0.01 level of probability, indicating thereby that the test is reliable.

Content Validity: In the process of constructions the knowledge test care was taken to include items covering all aspects with respect to knowledge about improved dairy farming practices and standardised methods were followed for selection of final knowledge test items. Hence, the score obtained by this tet measured none other than knowledge of the respondents as intended.

5. Scoring Technique

There were 20 items in the final tet which was adminstered to the respondents. Each correct response was given score '1' and '0' for wrong answers for all dichotomous items. For multiple choice questions the scoring was given as 3, 2 and 1 for most accurate, near to accurate and least accurate responses.

Dependent Variables

1. Role Performance

According to Sargent (1951) "a personal role is a pattern of type of social behaviour which seems situationally appropriate to him in terms of demands and expectations of these in his group." Linton (1945) defined role as "the sum total of the culture patterns associated with a particular status".

The role behaviour is the same as the concept of role performance, which according to Davis (1949) was "how an individual actually performs in a given position, as distinct from how he is supposed to perform". Rizvi (1967) defined job performance as the manner and extent to which different jobs are performed in practical situation.

For the present study role performance has been conceptualized as the various activities the rural women perform with regards to dairy farming practices.

A list of 23 roles was identified by interviewing 24 rural women 6 each from the four land size categories. These women were directly questioned as to indicate their roles which are being performed by them on dairying. These items were placed on three point continuum ranging from always to never and they were scored 3, 2 and 1 for always, sometimes and never responses respectively. Thus the maximum score one can attain was 69 whereas the minimum possible was 23.

2. *Perceived Training Needs*

Flippo (1966) defined training as the act of increasing the knowledge and skill of an employee for doing a particular job. Lynton and Pareek (1967) defined training as the process by which the desired knowledge, skill, attitude and ideas are inculcated and reinforced in an organism.

According to the dictionary of Psychology (1973) need is a condition marked by the feeling of lack or want of something or regaining of the performance of some action.

Leagans (1961) viewed need as the difference between "what is and what outht to be".

For the present study the perceived training need is operationalized as the respondent's feeling to have training in different areas of dairy farming. Perceived needs were determined by getting their responses to direct questions pertaining to different areas of dairy farming. Each item has been provided with two responses categories i.e. important and not important and score assigned were '1' and '0' respectively. In addition, opinions on duration, venue and appropriate time for training were also asceraine.

Data Collection

Development of tools, test and schedule preparation was undertaken in the period from December, 1988 to May, 1989.

According to nature of the study all the variables had been put in the form of questions for getting response from farm women. The comprehensive interview schedule covering the objectives of the study had been formulated for recording the responses of the respondents. The data collection work was carried out from June, 1989 to September, 1989. The respondents were individually interviewed by the researcher himself either at home or at their farms. The usual precaustions for interviewing the farm women were carefully observed to establish rapport and to create responsive situation for obtaining reliable information.

Statistical Methods Used

The statistical methods used in this study were frequencies, percentages, mean, standard deviation, 't' test, correlation coefficient and multiple regression analysis.

't' Test

The 't' test was applied in this study to test the signficance of mean values for any two variables within and between two districts.

Correlation Coefficient

Pearson's product moment correlation coefficient was computed by employing the formula suggested by Snedecar and Cochran (1967) to ascertain the relationship between socio-personal characteristics (independent variables) and the role performance and perceived training needs of the respondents.

Multiple Regression Analysis

In order to understand the influence of socio-personal and psychological characteristics on role performance and perceived training needs, multiple regression analysis was carried out.

4
RESULTS AND DISCUSSIONS

In the light of the objectives set forth for this study the data collected have been analysed by employing appropriate analytical techniques as given in the chapter Methodology. The results have been presented and discussed in this chapter under the following sections:

1. Profile of the farm women in different settings.
2. Identification of role of farm women and their role performance in dairy farming practices.
3. Time spend on dairy farming practices by farm women.
4. Level of knowledge or respondents regarding Breeding, Feeding, Management and Health care according to land holding categories.
5. Perceived training needs of farm women in respect of dairy farming practices and duration, time and place for farm women training.
6. Relational analysis of personal, communication and psychological variables with role performance and perceived training needs of the respondents regarding dairy farming practices.

Profile of the Farm Women in Different Settings

Age

Table 4.1 (i) revealed that majority of the respondents (above 60%) in all the settings namely Mahindergarh, Kurukshetra and overall fall in the middle age group. The lowest percentage of the farm women were in old age group i.e. 18, 19 and 17.5 in Mahendergarh, Kurukshetra and overall respectively. In different settings the low age group farm women were 21 per cent in Mahendergarh, 16 per cent in Kurukshetra and 19.5 per cent in overall sample. The mean age of the pooled sample was about 33 years and majority of the women were in the age group ranging from 24 to 42 years.

Table 4.1 : Profile of the Farm Women According to Their Personal Traits (Percentage)

(i) AGE

Settings	*Low*	*Medium*	*High*	*Mean*
Mahendergarh (N=100)	21	61	18	30.55
Kurukshetra (N=100)	16	65	19	34.93
Pooled (N=200)	19.5	63.0	17.5	32.74

Respondent's Education

Farm women under this study were categorised under illiterate, primary, middle, high school and above high school level of education. It is seen from the Table 4.1(ii) that higher the education level, lower is the distribution of the respondents. Not a single respondent was found to have above high school level of education in Mahendergarh district whereas in Kurukshetra district there were only three respondents who were educated upto high school and above high school.

Majority of the farm women, 41 per cent in Mahendergarh, 68 per cent in Kurukshetra and 54.5 per cent in pooled sample were found to be illiterate. As primary level of education is concerned, the

Table 4.1 : (ii) RESPONDENT'S EDUCATION

Settings	*Illiterate*	*Primary School*	*Middle School*	*High School*	*Above High School*
Mahendergarh (N=100)	41	35	17	07	00
Kurukshetra (N=100)	68	19	07	03	03
Pooled (N=200)	54.5	26.5	12.5	5.0	1.5

percentage of respondents who had primary level of education were 35, 19 and 26.5 in Mahendergarh, Kurukshetra and pooled sample respectively. In Mahendergarh the percentage of middle school educated respondents was more than in Kurukshetra district.

Family Education

Table 4.1(iii) showed that most of the farm women had the medium level of family education followed by high and low family education level. In Mahendergarh district 14 per cent, 72 per cent and 14 per cent respondents had low, medium and high family education level respectively. The corresponding figures for Kurukshetra district were 17, 60 and 23 respectively. In pooled sample equal percentage (17%) had been shared by low and high family education groups and there waş 66 per cent respondents in medium level of family education.

Table 4.1 : (iii) FAMILY EDUCATION

Settings	*Low*	*Medium*	*High*	*Mean*
Mahendergarh (N=100)	14	72	14	7.00
Kurukshetra (N=100)	17	60	23	5.10
Pooled (N=200)	17	66	17	6.07

Herd Size

Majority of the Farm women, 53 per cent in Mahendergarh, 46 per cent in Kurukshetra and 54 per cent in pooled were in medium herd size category. The large herd size were maintained by only 20, 19 and 20.5 per cent respondents in Mahendergarh, Kurukshetra and pooled respectively. The percentage of Farm women had low herd size in Mahendergarh, Kurukshetra and pooled were 27 per cent, 35 per cent and 25.5 per cent respectively. It was clear from the Table 4.1(iv) that a large number of respondents were rearing animals ranging from 4 to 10 and the mean herd size stood at 7 animals per family.

Milk Production

Maximum respondents were in medium level of milk production in Mahendergarh (70%), Kurukshetra (73%) and pooled (68%). The high level of milk production was attained only by respondents, 15

Table 4.1 : (iv) HERD SIZE

Settings	Low	Medium	High	Mean
Mahendergarh (N=100)	27	53	20	6.65
Kurukshetra (N=100)	35	46	19	6.70
Pooled (N=200)	25.5	54.0	20.5	6.70

per cent in Mahendergarh, 15 per cent farm women in Kurukshetra and 13.5 per cent in pooled sample. The percentage of respondents in low milk production category were 15, 12 and 18.5 in Mahendergarh, Kurukshetra and pooled sample respectively. A perusal of the Table 4.1(v) revealed that majority of the respondents were able to get milk production ranging anywhere between 6 to 8 litres per day. There were only few respondents who were getting milk beyond 18 litres per day from their animals.

Table 4.1 : (v) MILK PRODUCTION

Settings	Low	Medium	High	Mean
Mahendergarh (N=100)	15	70	15	14.52
Kurukshetra (N=100)	12	73	15	9.34
Pooled (N=200)	18.5	68.0	13.5	11.93

Milk Consumption

The figures in the Table 4.1 (vi) showed that a large number of respondents (27%) in Mahendergarh district was consuming about one litre of milk per day whereas in this low category of milk consumption there were only 17 per cent of respondents in Kurukshetra district. However, more than 50 per cent of the respondents were in medium milk consumption category in Mahendergarh, Kurukshetra and pooled

Table 4.1 : (vi) MILK CONSUMPTION

Settings	Low	Medium	High	Mean
Mahendergarh (N=100)	27	52	21	4.82
Kurukshetra (N=100)	17	62	21	5.30
Pooled (N=200)	12.5	68.0	19.5	5.07

sample. Twenty one per cent of respondents were consuming more milk (beyond 8 litre per day) in both the districts.

Milk Sale

Majority of the rural women, 68 per cent in Mahendergarh district were in the medium milk sale category whereas majority (64%) in Kurukshetra were in low group as stated in Table 4.1 (vii). There were very few respondents in low milk sale category in Mahendergarh district and in high milk sale category in Kurukshetra district. This clearly indicate that the respondents in Mahendergarh were involved more intensively in milk trade than their counterpart in Kurukshetra.

Table 4.1 : (vii) MILK SALE

Settings	*Low*	*Medium*	*High*	*Mean*
Mahendergarh (N=100)	17	68	15	9.68
Kurukshetra (N=100)	64	28	08	3.96
Pooled (N=200)	30.0	56.5	13.5	6.82

Family Size

The Table 4.1 (viii) depicted that the average family size of the pooled sample was found to be about 7. As high as 67 per cent of the respodents in Kurukshetra district had medium size of family whereas there were only 36 per cent in this category in Mahendergarh district. There were fewer respondents (14%) in low family sie category in Kurukshetra district as compare to 28 respondents in Mahendergarh district in the same category.

Table 4.1 : (viii) FAMILY SIZE

Settings	*Low*	*Medium*	*High*	*Mean*
Mahendergarh (N=100)	28	36	26	6.32
Kurukshetra (N=100)	14	67	19	6.69
Pooled (N=200)	21.0	59.5	19.5	6.51

Caste

The variable caste was quantified by adoptions the procedure developed by Trivedi (1963). The respondents were categorized into low, medium and high caste groups on the basis of mean and standard deviation. The findings indicated in Table 4.1 (ix) that majority of the respondents (37%) in Mahendergarh district belong to high caste group whereas majority (45%) of Kurukshetra district respondents belong to high caste group. The more or less equal number of respondents i.e. 32 per cent and 35 per cent are in low caste group in both the distícts, whereas in pooled sample it was 29 per cent.

Table 4.1 : (ix) CASTE

Settings	*Low*	*Medium*	*High*	*Mean*
Mahendergarh (N=100)	32	31	37	3.17
Kurukshetra (N=100)	35	20	45	4.05
Pooled (N=200)	29.0	48.5	22.5	3.85

Extension Contact

The extent of contact with the extension agencies was ascertained by interviewing the respondent. The findings presented a contrasting picture between Mahendergarh and Kurukshetra districts. In Mahendergarh 78 per cent of the respondents were found to have medium level of extension contact in contrast to 65 per cent respondents of Kurukshetra were maintaining a low extension contact. The number of respondents in high extension contact category in both the districts was not more than nine. From this, it could be concluded that the extension contact was low to moderate in both the districts (Table 4.1 (x).

Table 4.1 : (x) EXTENSION CONTACT

Settings	*Low*	*Medium*	*High*	*Mean*
Mahendergarh (N=100)	18	78	04	23.82
Kurukshetra (N=100)	65	26	09	6.07
Pooled (N=200)	29.5	41.0	29.5	14.94

Mass Media Exposure

The Table 4.1 (xi) also revealed the respondent's exposure to various sources of mass media such as magaines, radio, TV etc. Highest percentage of respondnets (79%) were in medium mass media exposure category in Kurukshetra district whereas 58 per cent of the respondents were in medium mass media exposure category in Mahendergarh.

Table 4.1 : (xi) MASS MEDIA EXPOSURE

Settings	*Low*	*Medium*	*High*	*Mean*
Mahendergarh (N=100)	22	58	20	2.57
Kurukshetra (N=100)	15	79	06	1.78
Pooled (N=200)	18.5	68.0	13.5	2.18

There was not much of a difference in the distribution of respondents in low and high mass media exposure categories in Mahendergarh district, whereas in Kurukshetra there were 15 per cent respondents in low exposure category as against 6 per cent in the high category. The mean mass media exposure of the pooled sample was 2.18 with little variation, indicating thereby that the mass media exposure was very low in the area.

Attitude towards Dairy Farming

Attitude of farm women towards dairy farming is quite often felt as essential pre-disposition for the success of dairy farming. Many a times, it is felt that dairying is one activity which is most suited for farm women. It is seen from the Table 4.1(xii) that majority of the farm women in all the three settings i.e. Mahendergarh district, Kurukshetra district and in pooled sample fall in the neutral level of

Table 4.1 : (xii) ATTITUDE TOWARDS DAIRY FARMING

Settings	*Unfavour-able*	*Neut-ral*	*Favour-able*	*Mean*
Mahendergarh (N=100)	24	60	16	18.16
Kurukshetra (N=100)	23	51	26	18.02
Pooled (N=200)	23.5	63.0	13.5	18.09

attitude towards dairy farming. There was not much of a difference in the distribution of respondents in Mahendergarh and Kurukshetra districts with about 60 per cent of them in the neutral category. However, there were more respondents in Kurukshetra district with favourable attitude towards dairy farming than in Mahendergarh.

In pooled sample as high as 63 per cent had neutral level, 23.5 per cent unfavourable and only 13.5 per cent had favourable level of attitude towards dairy farming. On the whole, it could be stated that the attitude of the respondents was neither favourable not unfavourable towards dairy farming.

Economic Motivation

It was found from the Table 4.1 (xiii) that 71 per cent respondents had medium level of economic motivation in Kurukshetra district whereas only 36 per cent respondents had medium level of economic motivation in Mahendergarh district. In case of pooled sample 52 per cent of respondents fall in medium category. 35 per cent of the respondents were in high economic motivation category in Mahendergarh whereas only 8 per cent were in Kurukshetra.

Table 4.1 : (xiii) ECONOMIC MOTIVATION

Settings	*Low*	*Medium*	*High*	*Mean*
Mahendergarh (N=100)	29	36	35	5.96
Kurukshetra (N=100)	21	71	08	6.79
Pooled (N=200)	43.0	52.0	5.0	6.88

Value Orientation (Conservatism-Progressivism)

Research indicated (Table 4.1 (xiv) that those people who oriented towards progressivism tend to be successful in their enterprises, compared to those whose outlook is towards conservatism. Hence, it was thought appropriate to include this variable in a study like this. The results indicated that the distribution of respondents in all the three categories was almost equal in Kurukshetra district. Though, the respondents in low category was same in all the three samples there were 43 per cent respondents with medium value orientation in Mahendergarh district.

Table 4.1 : (xiv) VALUE ORIENTATION (Conservatism–Progressivism)

Settings	*Low*	*Medium*	*High*	*Mean*
Mahendergarh (N=100)	36	43	21	18.95
Kurukshetra (N=100)	36	32	32	20.06
Pooled (N=200)	36.0	37.5	26.5	19.51

Level of Aspiration

It can be seen from the Table 4.1 (xv) that in Mahendergarh district 69 per cent respondents had medium level of aspiration whereas the rest were almost equally distributed in low and high categories of aspiration. In case of Kurukshetra district 23, 59 and 18 per cent respondents had low, medium and high level of aspiration respectively. In pooled sampie 63 respondents had medium level of aspiration, 19.5 per cent low level and 17.5 per cent had high level of aspiration. It can be revealed from the Table that majority of the farm women had medium level of aspiration.

Table 4.1 : (xv) LEVEL OF ASPIRATION

Settings	*Low*	*Medium*	*High*	*Mean*
Mahendergarh (N=100)	16	69	15	43.2
Kurukshetra (N=100)	23	59	18	46.25
Pooled (N=200)	19.5	63.0	17.5	44.63

Identification of Role of Farm Women and their Role Performance in Dairy Farming Practices

Identification of Role

After interviewing 24 farm women from non-sample area, 23 roles were identified which a farm women can perform in relation to dairy farming. The identified roles are as under :

1. Fodder harvesting.
2. Feeding to the animals.

3. Watering to the animals.
4. Carying fodder to home.
5. Chopping of fodder.
6. Grazing of animals.
7. Grinding of cattle feeds.
8. Purchase of cattle feeds.
9. Bathing of animals.
10. Making cow dung cakes.
11. Cleaning of sheds.
12. Weather protection of animals.
13. Drying of sheds.
14. Cleaning of mangers.
15. Grooming.
16. Milking of animals.
17. Care and heating of milk.
18. Churning of curd.
19. Selling of milk.
20. Care of newly born calf.
21. Care of sick animals.
22. Vaccination of animals.
23. Insemination of animals.

Role Performance

The success of any dairy farm irrespective of its sectors (either public, private or cooperative) and size (depending on cattle or buffalo heads with their followers) depends upon the efficacy and efficiency of role performance. Role performance of farm women in this study was carried out by obtaining responses on 23 specific dairying areas. The analysis of data depending upon these areas will be discussed here.

In order to know the distribution of respondents in different categorics of role performance the respondents are divided under low, medium and high levels on the basis of calculated mean and standard deviations. It can be very well observed from the Table 4.2 that a majority of the respondents occupied the middle level of role perfor-

Table 4.2 : Role Performance of Farm Women in Different Settings according to their Land Holdings

	Level of Role Performance		
	Low	*Medium*	*High*
MAHENDERGARH			
Landless (N=28)	2 (7.14)	23 (82.14)	3 (10.7)
Small (N=29)	1 (3.5)	28 (96.55)	0 (0.0)
Medium (N=23)	3 (13.0)	18 (78.2)	2 (8.6)
Large (N=20)	6 (30.0)	13 (65.0)	1 (5.0)
KURUKSHETRA			
Landless (N=34)	2 (5.9)	23 (67.6)	9 (26.4)
Small (N=22)	1 (4.5)	13 (59.1)	8 (36.3)
Medium (N=24)	2 (8.3)	20 (83.3)	2 (8.3)
Large (N=20)	6 (30.0)	13 (65.0)	1 (5.0)
POOLED SAMPLE			
Landless N=62)	4 (6.4)	48 (77.4)	10 (16.1)
Small (N=51)	1 (2.00)	45 (88.2)	5 (9.8)
Medium (N=47)	5 (10.6)	35 (74.4)	7 (15.0)
Large (N=40)	9 (22.5)	27 (67.5)	4 (10.0)

Figures in parenthesis shows percentage

mance. Mahendergarh district showed the largest majority of the respondents falling in the medium level of role performance with a distribution of about 82 per cent, 97 per cent, 78 per cent and 65 per cent respondents among landless, small, medium and large farmers respectively. The corresponding distributions in the Kurukshetra district and pooled samples were about 68 per cent, 59 per cent, 83 per cent and 65 per cent and 77 per cent, 88 per cent, 74 per cent and 68 per cent, respectively. Only few of the respondents in all the settings could occupy either high or low level of role performance. In Mahendergarh district even in case of role performance, not a single high performer found falling under the small land holding farm women. It was not due to any specific reason. The highest distribution of respondents recorded in all the settings was about 97 per cent in Mahendergarh among small land holders in medium level of role performance whereas 83 per cent of the respondents in medium land holding were in medium level of role performance in Kurukshetra.

Further, pooled sample 88 per cent of the small farmers had also medium level of role performance.

Time Spent on Dairy Farming Activities

The rural women are involved in various activities related to agriculture, dairying, cooking, care of the children etc. In this study an attempt was made to ascertain the time spent by the farm women on different activities in dairying. A list of 23 activities on dairy farming on which the rural women were spending their time was prepared. The respondents were asked to indicate the time spent in minutes per day on all these activities. The results are presented in Table 4.3 under four different categories such as fodder and feeding, management of animals, milking and processing of milk and health care of animals.

Table 4.3 Average Time Spent in Hrs./Day on Four Different Areas of Dairy Farming by Different Land Size Categories of Respondents in Mahendergarh and Kurukshetra

Average time spent in hrs. per day	Area				
	Fodder and feeding of animals	*Management of animals*	*Milking & processing of milk*	*Health care*	*Total*
Landless					
Mahendergarh	5.25	1.28	0.56	0.18	7.27
Kurukshetra	3.44	1.01	0.52	0.09	5.05
Small					
Mahendergarh	3.63	1.44	0.96	0.11	6.05
Kurukshetra	1.92	1.05	1.14	0.10	4.20
Medium					
Mahendergarh	3.90	1.70	1.34	0.19	7.01
Kurukshetra	1.39	0.85	1.49	0.11	3.80
Large					
Mahendergarh	3.67	1.56	1.21	0.15	6.57
Kurukshetra	1.39	1.28	1.92	0.13	4.67
Total					
Mahendergarh	4.15	1.48	1.00	0.15	6.70
Kurukshetra	2.22	1.03	1.16	0.10	4.50
Pooled	3.18	1.25	1.08	0.13	5.60

The findings indicated in Table 4.3 showed that the respondents were spending more time on fodder and feeding of animals. On an average each respondent was spending about 4.15 hrs. in Mahendergarh district and 2.22 hrs. in Kurukshetra district on feeding of animals. Next in order of importance were management of animals and, milking and processing of milk. On health care the rural women were spending very less time which ranged from 0.10 hrs./day in Kurukshetra district to 0.15 hrs./day in Mahendergarh district. The data also clearly indicated that on an average the respondents were spending 4.50 hrs. and 6.70 hrs. on dairying activities in Kurukshetra and Mahendergarh districts, respectively. This figure worked out to be 5.60 hrs. for pooled data which reflected the contribution of rural women in the field of dairy farming.

There was a marked difference in the time spent on fodder and feeding of animals between Mahendergarh and Kurukshetra's respondents. The detailed information provided in Table 4.3 clearly explains the differences.

On fodder and feeding of animals landless women were spending 5.25 hrs./day in Mahendergarh district compared to 3.44 hrs./day in Kurukshetra district. This difference was due to the fact that green fodder or weeds are easily available in Kurukshetra district whereas in Mahendergarh it is very difficult to collect green weeds and fodder for animals due to less rainfall and very less irrigation facilities as compared to Kurukshetra district.

Similarly respondents of small, medium and large farm categories were devoting more time (3.60 hrs./day) on fodder and feeding of animals in Mahendergarh district compared to their counterparts in Kurukshetra district.

On management of animals, maximum time was spent by the farm women of medium land size category in Mahendergarh distric whereas least time was devoted to this activity by the same category of farm women in Kurukshetra district.

As expected very less time was spent by landless women on milking and processing of milk in both the districts. Maximum time (1.92 hrs./day) was devoted to this activity by large land holding respondents of Kurukshetra district. The time spent on health-care activities ranged from 0.09 hrs./day to 0.19 hrs./day in both the districts put together.

The differences in the time spent on all the activities between the respondents of Mahendergarh and Kurukshetra were found significant as indicated by the 't' values except in milking of animals and care of the sick animals.

It can clearly be seen that except for the areas of milking of animals and care of sick animals; in all aspects, the respondents of both the districts differed significantly. The non-significant difference between the respondents in respect of these above mentioned areas is easily understandable because both milking and care of sick animals are such activities, which when taken care of; cannot be either postponed or left to some one else. One has to carry it out in was footing step until the responsibility is fully discharge. Therefore, findings showed a similarity among the respondents in connection with time spent in these two areas.

In the area of fodder and feeding of animals the activities which consumed maximum time of the respondents were fodder harvesting, feeding of animals and watering to animals in both the districts (Table 4.4). Similarly, bathing of animals and making cow dung cakes took away the time of farm women to a substantial extent in the area of management of animals. The respondents were found spending about half an hour per day in milking of animals and a little over quarter of an hour in care and heating of milk. Though time spent on health care was less, care of the newly born calf was an activity on which they were spending about five minutes in a day.

The time spent on health care activities was less because of the fact that these activities were to be performed once in a while by the women. For instance care of the newly born calf demands time only when there is a calf birth. Same is true in case of sick animal and other health care activities. In all the other three areas almost all the activities are regular in nature which need to be attended by the farm women daily and hence most of their time is spent on such activities.

As a result of commulative effect, it was observed that the time spent by the farm women of Mahendergarh district in overall activities is higher than those of Kurukshetra district and they showed a high level of significant difference (Table 4.3 and 4.4).

Frequency Distribution of Respondents on the Basis of Differential Level of Knowledge

Knowledge is an essential pre-requisite for efficient execution

Table 4.4 Activities on Which More Time was Spent by Rural Women

Sl. No.	Activity	Time Spent in mts./day		
		Mahendergarh	Kurukshetra	Pooled
I.	**FODDER & FEEDING**			
1.	Fodder Harvesting	74.40	30.50	52.40
2.	Feeding of Animals	59.00	40.20	49.60
3.	Watering to Animals	46.50	35.70	41.10
II.	**MANAGEMENT OF ANIMALS**			
1.	Bathing of animals	29.40	23.20	26.30
2.	Making cow dung cakes	22.00	13.50	17.80
3.	Cleaning of sheds	13.50	9.80	11.60
III.	**MILKING AND MILK PROCESSING**			
1.	Milking of animals	30.40	30.90	30.70
2.	Care and Heating of milk	14.30	20.20	17.20
3.	Churning of curd	11.70	16.60	14.10
IV.	**HEALTH CARE**			
1.	Care of newly born calf	5.60	3.50	4.60
2.	Care of sick animals	2.90	2.50	2.70

of activities. Therefore, for the success of any productive activity, impact of knowledge can not be ignored. It is more true in case of dairy farming. Because, the animals do not communicate as such, their problems and necessities are to be understood or realized and it is only knowledge which permits to do so. In order to examine the frequency distribution of farm women on differential level of knowledge in accordance with their land holdings; an attempt has been made to look it from breeding, feeding, management, health care and overall knowledge levels (Table 4.5).

Knowledge Level of Breeding

Majority of the respondents in all the three settings namely Mahendergarh, Kurukshetra and in pooled sample fell in the medium

Table 4.5: Differential Level of Knowledge of Farm Women in Mahendergarh, Kurukshetra and Pooled Sample Regarding Dairy Farming

	Knowledge Level of Breeding		
	Low	*Medium*	*High*
	(1)	(2)	(3)
Knowledge Level of BREEDING			
MAHENDERGARH			
Landless (N=28)	10 (35.7)	16 (57.1)	2 (7.1)
Small (N=29)	11 (37.9)	15 (51.7)	3 (10.3)
Medium (N=23)	8 (34.8)	11 (47.8)	4 (17.3)
Large (N=20)	4 (20.0)	12 (60.00)	4 (20.0)
KURUKSHETRA			
Landless (N=34)	12 (35.29)	18 (52.94)	4 (11.76)
Small (N=22)	9 (40.9)	12 (54.5)	1 (4.5)
Medium (N=24)	14 (58.3)	8 (33.3)	2 (8.3)
Large (N=20)	4 (20.0)	14 (70.0)	2 (10.0)
POOLED SAMPLE			
Landless N=62)	21 (33.8)	37 (59.67)	4 (6.4)
Small (N=51)	14 (27.4)	31 (60.7)	6 (11.8)
Medium (N=47)	7 (14.9)	35 (74.4)	5 (10.6)
Large (N=40)	10 (25.0)	24 (60.0)	6 (15.0)
Knowledge Level of FEEDING			
MAHENDERGARH			
Landless (N=28)	9 (32.1)	15 (53.5)	4 (14.3)
Small (N=29)	11 (37.9)	12 (41.37)	6 (33.7)
Medium (N=23)	9 (39.1)	9 (39.1)	5 (21.7)
Large (N=20)	7 (35.0)	11 (55.0)	2 (10.0)
KURUKSHETRA			
Landless (N=34)	28 (82.35)	2 (5.88)	4 (11.76)
Small (N=22)	13 (59.1)	3 (13.6)	6 (27.3)
Medium (N=24)	14 (58.3)	3 (12.5)	7 (29.1)
Large (N=20)	12 (60.0)	3 (15.0)	5 (25.0)

(contd.)

Table 4.5 (contd.)

	(1)	(2)	(3)
Knowledge Level of FEEDING (contd.)			
POOLED SAMPLE			
Landless N=62)	22 (35.5)	32 (51.61)	8 (12.9)
Small (N=51)	19 (37.25)	25 (49.02)	7 (13.72)
Medium (N=47)	18 (38.29)	22 (46.8)	7 (14.9)
Large (N=40)	13 (33.5)	18 (45.0)	9 (22.5)
Knowledge Level of MANAGEMENT			
MAHENDERGARH			
Landless (N=28)	11 (39.2)	14 (50.)	3 (10.7)
Small (N=29)	9 (31.0)	17 (58.6)	3 (10.3)
Medium (N=23)	7 (30.4)	14 (60.9)	2 (8.6)
Large (N=20)	8 (40.0)	8 (40.0)	4 (20.0)
KURUKSHETRA			
Landless (N=34)	17 (50.0)	14 (41.2)	3 (8.8)
Small (N=22)	8 (36.3)	13 (59.2)	1 (4.5)
Medium (N=24)	14 (58.3)	8 (33.3)	2 (8.2)
Large (N=20)	3 (15.0)	16 (80.0)	1 (5.0)
POOLED SAMPLE			
Landless N=62)	29 (46.7)	23 (37.09)	10 (16.12)
Small (N=51)	19 (37.2)	24 (47.05)	8 (15.7)
Medium (N=47)	13 (27.6)	25 (53.2)	9 (19.1)
Large (N=40)	14 (35.0)	15 (37.5)	11 (27.5)
Knowledge Level of HEALTH CARE			
MAHENDERGARH			
Landless (N=28)	24 (85.7)	2 (7.1)	2 (7.1)
Small (N=29)	13 (40.8)	8 (29.6)	8 (29.6)
Medium (N=23)	12 (52.1)	8 (34.8)	3 (13.0)
Large (N=20)	7 (35.0)	9 (45.0)	4 (20.0)
KURUKSHETRA			
Landless (N=34)	21 (61.76)	12 (35.29)	1 (2.94)
Small (N=22)	1 (4.5)	13 (59.1)	8 (36.3)
Medium (N=24)	11 (45.83)	10 (41.66)	3 (12.5)
Large (N=20)	3 (15.0)	17 (85.0)	0 (0.0)

(contd.)

Table 4.5 (contd.)

	(1)	(2)	(3)
Knowledge Level of HEALTH CARE (contd.)			
POOLED SAMPLE			
Landless N=62)	26 (41.93)	33 (53.22)	4 (4.83)
Small (N=51)	18 (35.3)	28 (55.0)	5 (9.8)
Medium (N=47)	10 (21.3)	32 (68.08)	5 (10.6)
Large (N=40)	9 (22.5)	24 (60.0)	7 (17.5)
OVERALL Level of Knowledge			
MAHENDERGARH			
Landless (N=28)	10 (35.7)	17 (60.7)	1 (3.6)
Small (N=29)	10 (34.5)	16 (55.1)	3 (10.3)
Medium (N=23)	5 (21.7)	14 (60.9)	4 (17.3)
Large (N=20)	5 (25.0)	13 (65.0)	2 (10.0)
KURUKSHETRA			
Landless (N=34)	20 (59.0)	12 (35.29)	2 (5.88)
Small (N=22)	7 (31.8)	14 (63.6)	1 (4.5)
Medium (N=24)	5 (20.83)	14 (58.3)	5 (20.83)
Large (N=20)	3 (15.0)	16 (80.0)	1 (5.0)
POOLED SAMPLE			
Landless N=62)	18 (29.0)	42 (67.7)	2 (3.2)
Small (N=51)	19 (37.25)	23 (45.09)	9 (17.6)
Medium (N=47)	14 (8.5)	26 (55.3)	7 (14.9)
Large (N=40)	9 (22.5)	26 (65.0)	5 (12.5)

Figures in parenthesis shows percentage

level of knowledge about breeding. Their distributions in Mahendergarh district were about 57, 51, 48 and 60 per cent among landless, small, medium and large land holding farm women, respectively. The corresponding distribution in medium level of knowledge about breeding in Kurukshetra district and pooled samples were about 53%, 55%, 33%, 70% and about 60%, 61%, 74% and 60% respectively. The medium level was followed by distribution of respondents in low and high level of knowledge regarding breeding. It is unfortunate that only few respondents occupied the higher level of knowledge about breeding in al the three settings. The respective distributions of respondents in the farm land holding categories namely landless, small, medium and large were about 7%, 10%, 17% and 20% in Mahendergarh district; about 12%, 5%, 8% and 10% in Kurukshetra district and about 6%, 12%, 11% and 15% in the pooled sample respectively.

Knowledge Level of Feeding

Similar trend was found even in case of distribution of respondents in medium level of knowledge about feeding in Mahendergarh district. To be precise; about 54%, 41%, 39% and 55% of the farm women were falling in the medium level among the landless, small, medium and large land holding group of farm women respectively. The scenario was however different in Kurukshetra district. In the lower level of knowledge regarding feeding; majority of the respondents found their places among the landless, small, medium and large land holding farm women. Their distribution was about 82%, 59%, 58% and 60% respectively. In the pooled sample, distinct demarcation of distribution of farm women was not found. About 87, 86, 85 and 77 per cent of them among landless, small, medium and large land holding occupied low to medium level of knowledge about feeding of dairy animals. Among the two districts however, medium level of knowledge was followed by low and high groups in Mahendergarh district while low level was found in Kurukshetra district followed by high and medium level of knowledge about feeding.

Knowledge Level of Management

In Mahendergarh, Kurukshetra as well as in pooled sample, majority of the respondents occupied the medium level of knowledge about management of dairy animals. In accordance with the landless, small, medium and large land holdngs the distributioins in medium level of farm women in Mahendergarh district were about 50, 59, 61 and 40 per cent in Kurukshetra district about 41, 59, 33 and 80 per cent and in pooled sample about 37, 47, 53 and 38 per cent respectively. In all the settings again majority were in medium level followed by low and high level of knowledge about management practices (Table 4.5).

Knowledge Level of Health Care

The Table 4.5 shows that there was no change in the trend of distribution of respondents in different levels depending upon their knowledge about health care in Kurukshetra district and in pooled sample. In accordance with the distribution, majority of respondents were in medium level of knowledge was followed by low and high level of knowledge about health care in the above mentioned two settings. As such it is similar to that of distribution of farm women in the context of their knowledge level about breeding and management. But, as far as Mahendergarh district was concerned, in the low level of knowledge about health care majority of the respondents identified themselves. Their distributions in accordance with the landless, small, medium and learge land holdings were about 86, 50, 52 and 35 per cent respectively. There is only about corresponding distribution of 14, 60, 48 and 65 per cent of the farm women occupying medium to high level of knowledge regarding health care. Coming to the distribution of farm women in Kurukshetra district and in the pooled samples, the medium level occupied about 35, 59, 42 and 85 per cent and 53, 55, 68 and 60 per cent respectively among landless, small, medium and large farm women.

Overall Level of Knowledge

A glimpse about the overall distribution of respondents in high, medium and low levels of knowledge has already been given in the Table 4.5. But, after analysing the distribution of respondents in different components of knowledge level among different land holding categories of farm women, it was felt necessary to verify the same distribution inaccordance with the land holdings. Though there was no specific trend of distribution of farm women among different categories of land holdings with respect to their level of knowlege, it was observed that in all the three settings namely Mahendergarh, Kurukshetra and in pooled sample, majority of the respondents occupied the medium level of knowledge followed by low and high level of knowledge (Table 4.5). In accordance with the landless, small, medium and large land holdings the distributions of respondents in Mahendergarh in the medium level were about 61, 55, 61 and 65 per cent in Kurukshetra, about 35, 64, 58, and 50 per cent and in the pooled sample about 68, 45, 55 and 65 per cent respectively. What came out as a matter of concern about finding is that a large number of respondents in all the settings had lower level of overall knowledge about dairy farming. Their distribution in accordance with landless, small, medium and large land holdings categories were about 36, 35, 22 and 25 per cent in Mahendergarh, about 59, 32, 21 and 30 per cent in Kurukshetra and about 29, 37, 9 and 23 per cent respectively in pooled sample were found in the low level of knowledge in overall.

Perceived Training Needs of Farm Women in Respect of Dairy Farming Practices and Duration, Time and Place for Farm Women Training

Perceived Training Needs of Farm Women in Different Settings According to their Land Holdings

Any change towards unpliftment is dependent upon the skill and ability of individuals. A continuous kind of improvement in an individual in respect of his performance can only be brought by training. Training equips an individual with knowledge, skill and ability but the crucial point in the training is to identify the content and number of individuals who felt the need of training. To be effective as well as productive, training should be based on needs. It should be neither persuasive nor imposed. Therefore, it was attempted to know the training needs of the farm women in Mahendergarh and Kurukshetra districts of Haryana State. The respondents of the study were categories under low, medium and high level of training needs based on mean and standard deviations of the scores obtained by the respondents in this context.

The Table 4.6 indicates that the majority of the respondents occupied the medium level of training needs in all the three settings. The medium level of training needs observed among landless, small, medium and large land holding farm women was about 75, 55, 91 and 75 per cent in Mahendergarh district whereas 79, 96, 75 and 85 per cent in Kurukshetra district. In case of pooled sample about 69, 65, 87 and 75 per cent were in medium level of needs in different categories respectively. The distribution of respondents falling in the low and high training needs was almost equal ranging from 4 per cent to 20 per cent respectively. Nevertheless the distribution of respondents in low training needs level among landless, small, medium and large land holding farm women was about 11, 31, 9 and 5 per cent in Mahendergarh district and about 12, 0, 8 and 10 per cent in Kurukshetra district. In pooled sample about 11, 18, 4 and 5 per cent were in low level of training needs respectively. Likewise the corresponding distribution of respondents of high level of training needs in the context of the above mentioned four categories of land holdings farm women was about 14, 14, 0 and 20 per cent in Mahendergarh,

Table 4.6 Perceived Training Needs of Farm Women in Different Settings According to Their Land Holdings

	Level of Training Needs		
	Low	*Medium*	*High*
MAHENDERGARH			
Landless (N=28)	3 (10.7)	21 (75.0)	4 (14.3)
Small (N=29)	9 (31.0)	16 (55.1)	4 (13.8)
Medium (N=23)	2 (8.6)	21 (91.3)	0 (0.0)
Large (N=20)	1 (5.0)	15 (75.0)	4 (20.0)
KURUKSHETRA			
Landless (N=34)	4 (11.7)	27 (79.4)	3 (8.8)
Small (N=22)	0 (0.0)	21 (95.5)	1 (4.5)
Medium (N=24)	2 (8.3)	18 (75.0)	4 (16.6)
Large (N=20)	2 (10.0)	17 (85.0)	1 (5.0)
POOLED SAMPLE			
Landless N=62)	7 (11.3)	43 (69.3)	12 (19.3)
Small (N=51)	9 (17.6)	33 (64.7)	9 (17.6)
Medium (N=47)	2 (4.2)	41 (87.2)	4 (8.5)
Large (N=40)	2 (5.0)	30 (75.0)	8 (20.0)

Figures in parenthesis shows percentage

about 9, 5, 17 and 5 per cent in Kurukshetra. In pooled sample it was nearby 19, 18, 9 and 20 per cent respectively. Non-availability of a single respondent in the high level of training needs among medium land holders in Mahendergarh and in low group among small land holders in Kurukshetra is merely incidental. There is no specific reason for such a finding.

Perceived Training Needs of Farm Women on Different Sub-areas of Dairy Farming

Rearing of dairy animals and care and management of these animals by house wives go with the tradition of Indian society. Though it is not a part of this study to go back to the history and see how old the tradition is; the fact reamains that dairying animals including cattle and buffaloes are still considered as the poor man's insurance. But the concept of mdernization, rapid population growth and above all gradual fall in the per capita availability of grazing land almost forced the farmers to adopt intensive farming. As a result, there exists rapid technological growth to cope with the gradual increased demands for milk and milk products, all of sudden (within a span of few years) leaving our majority of the illiterate to low by educated farmers particularly the women folk far behind. But, as said earlier, keeping of dairy animals in most of the cases particularly in the North Western part of the country in general and the area under investigation is still felt as the responsibility of the women section rather than their counterparts. In the recent years, therefore, a sense of incompatibility developed gradually among the farm women in the context of organizing the improved dairy animals. It is in this context, that an attempt was made to identify where mostly the perceived training needs of farm women in the dairy farming practices.

As the Table 4.7 shows, among the five areas of dairy farming, farm women mostly interested in both the settings as well as in the pooled sample showed ther top most preference for training on health care of dairy animals. It is understandable, because,

a) everytime the farm women do not get the helping hand of veterinarians or field assistants when they are in need and their animals are sick;

b) due to cross breeding and induction of improved blood (genetic potential) of our animals though the productivity the disease resistence capacity has gone gown; and

c) due to rapid environmental polution may be, these are frequent occurances of uncommon diseases among the dairy animals.

Handling the diseased animals in the only area which is really unmanageable for farm women and they really fell helpless and let down. Therefore, to prefer training the most in this area is natural. In all the sub-areas of health care namely knowledge of common diseases, deworming of calves, precaution of contagious diseases and first aid treatments, they almost put equal importance. However, even among thus knowledge of common diseases got the first priority. It may be a result of their enthusiasm atleast try to manage their animals in the face of common diseases.

Similarly, in both the district as well as in the pooled sample, breeding was placed second by the farm women in the context

Table 4.7 : Perceived Training Needs of Farm Women in Different Sub-areas of Dairy Farming Practices

Sub-Areas & Practices	Mahendergarh			Kurukshetra			Pooled	
	Freq.	Mean	Rank	Freq.	Mean	Rank	Mean	Rank
A : BREEDING								
1. Selection of animals	83			85				
2. Identification of Heat Symptoms	85	65.7	II	85	63.0	II	64.3	II
3. Time of Insemination	76			77				
4. Breeding Efficiency	19			05				
B : FEEDING								
1. Feeding of newly born calf	86			85				
2. Feeding of young stock	80			80				
3. Feeding of milch animals	81			83				
4. Balance feeds and its composition	63	57.4	III	53	48.2	IV	52.8	III
5. Feeding of pregnant animals	46			16				
6. Feeding of heifers	26			13				
7. Feeding of dry animals	20			08				
C : MANAGEMENT								
1. Care at calving	83			84				
2. Care of newly born calf	83			84				
3. Clean milk production	67			54				
4. Dehorning of calf	66			72				
5. Management of cattle shed	47	52.2	IV	78	48.7	III	50.4	IV
6. Care of pregnant animals	45			19				
7. Care of heifers	25			14				
8. Watering to animals	53			32				
9. Castration	2			2				

Contd.

Table 4.7 : (contd.)

Sub-Areas & Practices	*Mahendergarh*			*Kurukshetra*			*Pooled*	
	Freq.	*Mean*	*Rank*	*Freq.*	*Mean*	*Rank*	*Mean*	*Rank*
D : <u>FODDER PRODUCTION</u>								
1. Rotation of fodder crops	30			--				
2. Land preparations	18			--				
3. Improved Varieties	24			--				
4. Fertilizer dose	21	28.0	V	--	--	V	14.0	V
5. Irrigation and Harvesting	23			--				
6. Conservation of Fodder	52			--				
E : <u>HEALTH CARE</u>								
1. Knowledge of common diseases	84			86				
2. Deworming of calf	84			85				
3. Precautions against contagious diseases	83	83.0	I	83	84.0	I	83.5	I
4. First aid treatment	81			82				

Freq. = Frequency

perceived training needs. It is judicious because, breeding is an area which is crucial for long term economy of dairy farming. Among the four sub-areas of breeding except on breeding efficienty all other three were required as important by the respondents. Even among the three aspects very judicious, identification of heat symptoms was preferred the most followed by selection of animals and time of insemination. Getting lower preference to breeding efficiency may be accounted to the fact that even if the farm women get training, the breeding efficiency is not an area which can be controlled by them.

With respect to feeding of dairy animals, though it stood as third ranked perceived training needs of farm women in the pooled sample; its perceptions were different in both the districts. While in Mahendergarh district it was placed third, in Kurukshetra district it stood fourth. The reason in this case may be a consequence of the fact that dairying in Mahendergarh district mostly in a primary occupation while in Kurukshetra district it is a secondary one. Therefore, realisation of the fact that economy of dairy farming depends upon feeding of animals in more in Mahendergarh district rather than in Kurukshetra. This fact is also emphasized by the results shown in respect of fodder production. Not a single respondent was found to perceive the need for training in any of the sub-areas of fodder production in Kurukshetra district. As a result fodder production in all the situations was ranked fifth. With respect to feeding, out of the total of 7 sub-areas, only four of them were preferred as important by the farm women in both the districts—namely; feeding of newly born calf, feeding of young stock, feeding of milch animals and composition of balanced feeding. However, in case of fodder production only conservation of fodder that too in Mahendergarh district was felt as important area for training by the respondents.

Though in the pooled sample management in totality was ranked fourth; the respondents of Kurukshetra district preferred it more even their counterparts in Mahendergarh district, and as a result in both the district, they ranked it as a subject of third and fourth priorities respectively. However, in both the districts care at calving and care of newly born calf were profound as the most needed training, followed by dehorning of calf and clean milk production. Neverthe-less, it can be seen from the Table that with respect of management of cattle shed and care of pregnant animals the farm women in both the districts differed a lot. It may be accounted to the situational factors once again. Because, dairying bring a primary occupation in Mahendergarh district they are relatively well versed with the aspects of cattle shed management and as such do not need much training, while in case of Kurukshetra district, it is other way around. Secondary scarcity of water in Mahendergarh district in comparison to Kurukshetra district gave vise to a sense of need to learn the aspects of water management and that is why the farm women of Mahendergarh district wanted to have training on watering of animals.

Frequency Distribution of Farm Women on the Basis of their Preference for Duration, Time and Place of Training Programme

The results in the Table 4.8 showed that five days training programme had preferred by most of the farm women in both the districts as well as in the pooled sample. In Mahendergarh, 56 per cent

Table 4.8 : Frequency Distribution of the Farm Women on the basis of their preference for the duration, time and place of training programmes

Settings	Duration				
	3 days	5 days	7 days	No Response	
Mahendergarh	8	56	21	15	
Kurukshetra	40	42	08	10	
Pooled	48	98	29	25	
	Time				
	Jan.	Feb.	March	June	No Response
Mahendergarh	26	06	42	11	15
Kurukshetra	05	00	58	27	10
Pooled	31	06	100	38	25
	Place				
	Vill.	Block	Distt.	NDRI*	No Response
Mahendergarh	30	32	19	04	15
Kurukshetra	31	59	00	00	10
Pooled	61	91	19	04	25

*NDRI = National Dairy Research Institute

farm ining for 5 days duration, only 21 and 8 per cent and 3 days duration respectively. In Kurukshetra distı ladies viewed that training programme should be c and 42 per cent opined that 5 days training prog ıitable. Going for the reasoning of this finding atleast revealed two to three very crucial issues. (a) They were not in a position to afford more time for training at stretch; (b) they also realised that lot were to be learned with regard to dairy farming; (c) may be they wanted to be at home by atleast at week ends. Researchers' experience at the time of data collection revealed that farm women's daily life was full of different kind of activities. They complete their household daily activities with great difficulties. There were some extra load of work which used to get postponed till the weak ends and farm women had to perform them like washing clothes, repairing chulahas, rearranging things and so on. Because, by week ends, they used to get helping hands from male counterparts and school going children.

The results in Table 4.8 indicates that majority, 42 per cent in Mahendergarh and 58 per cent in Kurukshetra district of Farm women had preferred month of March for trianing programmes. In Mahendergarh, 26 per cent preferred January and 11 per cent in June, whereas, in Kurukshetra, June had been preferred by 27 per cent of the farm women for organising the training programme. Getting preference for March month as the best time for training may be due to the two possible reasons; (a) weather conditions are the best in those days and (b) they remain relatively free from many other kind of agricultural activities.

It could be observed from the Table that most of the farm women 32 per cent in Mahendergarh and 59 per cent in Kurukshetra wanted that training programme should be organised at block headquarter. Village as a place of training programme had been preferred by 30 per cent and 31 per cent in Mahendergarh and Kurukshetra districts respectively. Only 4 per cent ladies from Mahendergarh had opined that national Dairy Research Institute should be the place for training programme. Entire farm women belonging to Kurukshetra district preferred that training programme should be organised either at village or block headquarter only.

The above findings were supported by Pawar (1979), Saroj (1988) and Omprakash (1988).

Relational Analysis of Personal, Communication and Psychological Variables with Role Performance and Perceived Training Needs of the Respondents Regarding Dairy Farming Practices

Relational Analysis of Personal Variables with Role Performance

After studying the role performance of the farm women it was thought appropriate to analyse the variables which influence the role performance. The information on the important variables associated with role performance helps in manipulating such variables to improve the role performance. The data were subjected to correlational and multiple regression analysis separately for both the districts as well as for the pooled data. The results are presented district wise.

Mahendergarh District

The results of relational analysis are presented in Table 4.9. The variables which had high inter correlations among themselves were scrutinized and one out of the two were eliminated to reduce the

Table 4.9 : Regression Analysis of Role Performance of Respondents of Mahendergarh District

Sl.No.	*Variable*	*r*	*b*	*t*
1.	Age	–.3132**	–.0578	.1144
2.	Education	.1953*	.8256	.7134
3.	Family Education	–.0014	–.1983	.3528
5.	Land Size	–.1591	–.1071	.2608
9.	Family Size	–.3434**	–1.0910	.4276
10.	Caste	–.1709	–.4158	.6735
13.	Extension Contact	.2461*	.0926	.0497
14.	Mass Media Exposure	–.1284	–.9252	.5220
15.	Attitude towards dairy farming	.1655	.5830	.3451
16.	Economic motivation	–.0913	–.3492	.6981
17.	Value Orientation	.1261	.3071	.1567
18.	Aspiration	.1111	.0382	.0541
23.	Knowledge	.0426	–.0270	.1108

R^2 = 0.2875 F value for R = 2.67*

* = Significant at 0.05 level of probability

** = Significant at 0.01 level of probability

multicollinerity effect. For instance variables herd size, was eliminated which was found having high correlation with land size. Similarly milk production, consumption and sale were also eliminated for a similar reason. The rest 13 variables were utilized for relational analysis. The findings of correlational analysis revealed that age, education, family size, and extension contact were found significantly related with the role performance. Out of these four, age and family size were negatively correlated whereas the other two were positively related with the role performance.

All the 13 variables were incorporated in multiple regression analysis to study the contribution of each of these variables to the role performance. However, a not a single variable was found exerting its contribution to the dependent variable in the presence of other variables. The multiple R^2 (0.2875) though small the 'F' value for 'R' was found significant.

Later all the variables which were significantly correlated with role performance and variables with high 't' values were incorporated in the model and by the process of elimination finally six variables were selected. The data presented in Table 4.10 indicated that family size, and extension contact were the two variables which were found to have significant correlation as well as regression coefficients. Education though found significantly related to role performance failed to show its contribution to a significant level. Similarly mass

Table 4.10 : Regression Analysis of Role Performance of Respondents of Mahendergarh District

Sl.No.	*of Variable*	*r*	*b*	*t*
2.	Education	.1953*	.6194	1.3551
9.	Family Size	–.3434**	–1.3740	4.2817**
13.	Extension Contact	.2461*	.1202	2.6455**
14.	Mass Media Exposure	–.1284	–.9469	1.9857*
15.	Attitude Towards Dairy Farming	.1655	.6027	1.9142
17.	Value Orientation	.1261	.3290	2.2253*

R^2 = 0.2611 F value for R = 5.48

* = Significant at 0.05 level of probability

** = Significant at 0.01 level of probability

media exposure and value orientation though not independently related to the role performance, could prove their contribution in the presence of other variables. Attitude towards dairy farming was not significantly related to role performance since higher 'r' value showed its contribution towards role performance. All these variables could explain a variation of about 26 per cent in the variation of role performance of respondents. The 'F' value for 'R' was found to be highly significant.

Education of the respondent was positively related to her role performance. Higher the education better was the perception of the incumbents' role which might be responsible for this positive relationship. However, its contribution to role performance was below the level of statistical significance. However, Jaswant Kaur (1981) observed significantly negative correlation.

The variable family size was negatively related as well as contributing significantly to the role performance. From this it could be inferred that a respondent with more family members was contributing less to her role when compared to an incumbent with fewer members in her family. The logical explanation could be that when the members were more in a family it was quite likely that they share their responsibilities and as such the role performance of an individual family member would be less than an individual who was to perform all the roles for want of members in her family.

Mass media exposure was observed to have negative regression coefficient which was significant at 5 per cent level. Its contribution was negative in the sense that higher the mass media exposure lesser was the contribution to the role performance of dairy farming activities. The reason could be that a woman who spent more time in reading magazines and viewing televisions or hearing radio naturally must be rich enough to employ the labourers for getting the work done and as such her role performance was low. Similarly a landless woman would be involving herself more in activities of dairying which being her livelihood and might be exposed less to the mass media.

Value orientation had a significant and positive coefficient thereby showing its importance in its contirbution to the role performance. The role performance depend on the degree of progressivism. The findings of Jaswant Kaur (1981) were contradicting the above findings.

Kurukshetra District

A similar approach which was adopted to analyse the data of Mahendergarh district was followed for the data of Kurukshetra district. In the first instance 14 variables were utilized for relational analysis. Among these variables seven were found significantly correlated with the role performance of farm women in Kurukshetra district. All these seven variables, family education, land size, milk consumption, caste, extension contact, value orientation and aspiration were negatively related to the role performance. None of the variables could exert their influence on the role performance. The results of the regressions and this also revealed that none of the 14 variables could contribute significantly to the dependent variable (Table 4.11).

The variables which had significant correlation coefficients were subjected to multiple regression analysis to find out few signifi-

Table 4.11 : Regression Analysis of Role Performance of Respondents of Kurukshetra District

Sl.No. of Variable		*r*	*b*	*t*
1.	Age	–.0647	–.0326	.0784
2.	Education	–.0916	.0992	.3809
3.	Family Education	–.2426*	–.1872	.2809
5.	Land Size	–.3360**	–.0954	.1609
7.	Milk consumption	–.3291**	–.0938	.2185
9.	Family Size	.0201	.1792	.2877
10.	Caste	–.3837**	–.6102	.4871
13.	Extension Contact	–.2106*	–.0383	.0642
14.	Mass Media Exposure	–.0990	–.4027	.9923
15.	Attitude towards dairy farming	.0700	.4185	.3005
16.	Economic motivation	–.0924	–.2269	.6257
17.	Value Orientation	–.2363*	–.1892	.1261
18.	Aspiration	–.2891**	–.0010	.0572
23.	Knowledge	–.0052	.2381	.1397

R^2 = 0.2474 F value for R = 2.00*

* = Significant at 0.05 level of probability

** = Significant at 0.01 level of probability

cant variables. The results (Table 4.12) indicated that none of the variables had significant regression coefficients. This implied that in Kurukshetra district the personal variables of the respondents could not contribute significantly to the variation in the role performance. The result of this district presented an entirely different pictures than that of Mahendergarh district owing to their situational differences as already explained in the methodology chapter.

Table 4.12 : Regression Analysis of Role Performance of Respondents of Kurukshetra District

Sl.No.	*of Variable*	*r*	*b*	*t*
3.	Family Education	–.2426*	–.1349	.5880
5.	Land Size	–.3360**	–.0790	.5249
7.	Milk Consumption	–.3291**	–.1456	.7630
10.	Caste	–.3837**	–.6426	1.5217
13.	Extension Contact	–.2106*	–.0304	.4991
17.	Value Orientation	–.2363*	–.1152	.9642
18.	Aspiration	–.2891**	.0355	.6940

R^2 = 0.1814 F value for R = 2.91

* = Significant at 0.05 level of probability

** = Significant at 0.01 level of probability

Jaswant Kaur (1981) had not confirm the above findings. She observed negative significant relationship with education and land holding size was positively and significantly related with the role performance.

Pooled Sample

After measuring the role performance of the rural women it was thought appropriate to analyse its relationship with personal characteristics of the respondents. In the first instance all the variables were subjected to correlational analysis. The variables which were highly correlated were identified. To reduce the multicollinearity effect some of the variables which the high inter correlations were not included in the regression analysis. For instance herd size and land size were highly correlated and hence herd size was not included in the analysis. Similarly, milk consumption was included which was found to have high correlation with milk production as well as milk sale and were deleted. In the process 14 variables were subjected to the multiple regression analysis. The results are presented in Table 4.13.

Table 4.13 : Regression Analysis of Role Performance of Respondents of Pooled Sample

Sl.No. of Variable	*r*	*b*	*t*
1. Age	–.2685**	–.957	1.4646
2. Education	.1295	.2874	.7944
3. Family Education	.0126	–.0958	.4333
5. Land Size	–.2312*	–.0972	.6317
7. Milk consumption	–.2620**	–.1384	.6318
9. Family Size	–.2036*	–.3062	1.1889
10. Caste	–.2785**	–.7299	1.8608
13. Extension Contact	.2584**	.0845	2.6126**
14. Mass Media Exposure	.1494	–.2201	0.5424
15. Attitude towards dairy farming	.1315	.3562	1.5950
16. Economic motivation	–.1910	–.7372	1.7148
17. Value Orientation	–.0623	–.0451	0.4590
18. Aspiration	–.0833	.0101	0.2597
23. Knowledge	.0300	.0044	0.0535

R^2 = 0.2398 F value for R = 4.17
* = Significant at 0.05 level of probability
** = Significant at 0.01 level of probability

A scrutiny of the above table showed that six variables were found significantly correlated with role performance of rural women. These were age, land size, milk consumption, family size, caste and extension contact. Out of these variables barying the last one, the rest were all associated negatively with the role performance.

The age of the respondent was found negatively correlated with role performance to a significant level. This means the level of role performance decreases with increase in the age of the respondent. The reason for this negative relationship is not beyond anybody's comprehension. When the rural lady becomes older and older, her performance obviously goes down especially in agriculture and dairy development activities. The findings of the study were in confirmity with study of Jaswant Kaur (1981).

The land size was also found negatively related to the role performance. This implies that the rural women who own more land perform less in dairy farming activities compared to their counterparts who own less or no land. It is reasonable to believe that the respondents who own more land depend upon hired labour in getting most of the dairy farming activities done as they can afford to hire the labour. It is very common in the villages that ladies with more land size do not go for fodder harvesting, carrying the fodder, milking the animals, preparation of dung cakes etc. In contrast a landless rural woman has to perform almost all the dairy farming activities. A similary analogy holds good for the significant and negative relationship between milk consumption and role performance. The consumption of milk was positively related to the land size of the respondents (R = 0.757).

The family size was found negatively influencing the role performance of the farm women. In families with more number of people the activities gets distributed among them and hence the performance of farm woman especially in agriculture and dairy farming activities is very likely to be decreased. On the contrary in nuclear families especially with fewer family members the rural women is likely to be involved in more activities and naturally her performance on these activities tend to be high.

Caste of the respondents was also found influencing the role performance in the negative direction. Because of cultural differences high caste people do not perform certain dairy farming activities like grazing of animals, fodder harvesting, carrying of fodder, making dung cakes, cleaning of sheds etc. Similarly low caste people by virtue of their low socio-economic profile are forced to some extent to perform many of the dairy farming activities.

The only variable which was found positively correlated with role performance was extension contact. Higher the extension contact more was the performance. It was quite likely that the farm women having more contact with extension personnel involved in dairy development work will learn more about dairying and hence perform better in their day to day work.

However, when all these variables were subjected to multiple regression analysis only extension contact was found to have significant and positive regression coefficient. All these 14 variables could explain a variation of about 24 per cent in the dependent variables.

With a view to find out the very important contributors to the more performance of the respondents only five variables with high 't' values were subjected to the regression analysis again. The results were presented in Table 4.14.

Table 4.14 : Regression Analysis of Role Performance of Respondents of Pooled Sample

Sl.No. of Variable		r	b	t
1.	Age	–.2685**	–.1420	2.9428**
10.	Caste	–.2785**	–1.0747	4.5408**
13.	Extension Contact	.2584*	0.0783	2.5997**
15.	Attitude Towards Dairy Farming	.1315	0.2311	1.1359
16.	Economic Motivation	–.1910	–0.6169	1.5090

R^2 = 0.2114 F value for R = 10.40
* = Significant at 0.05 level of probability
** = Significant at 0.01 level of probability

The findings indicatedthat age and caste of the respondents were found significantly and negatively contributing to their role performance. Whereas extension contact was observed to have a significant and positive regression coefficient. However, attitude towards dairy farming and economic motivation failed to exert their influence to a significant extent. The multiple R^2 value was 0.2114 and its 'F' value was found highly significant. These five variables could explain a variation of about 21 per cent compared to 24 per cent when there were 14 variables.

The findings of the relational analysis clearly brought out that age, caste and extension contact were very important contributors of role performance of rural ladies. The above findings contradicts the findings of Jaswant Kaur (1981).

Regression Analysis of Training Needs of Respondents

The training needs of the respondents vary from district to district depending their involvement in dairying, knowledge on various activities of dairying, situational factors etc. Hence, after analysing the training needs of farm women it was thought essential to identify the factors associated with the perception of training needs by the respondents. The data were analysed separately for both the districts and the results are given in Table 4.15.

Table 4.15 : Regression Analysis of Training Needs of Respondents of Mahendergarh District

Sl.No.	of Variable	*r*	*b*	*t*
1.	Age	–.1824	–.1370	1.3981
2.	Education	.1055	.8222	1.3447
3.	Family Education	–.1591	–.5798	1.9170
5.	Land Size	–.0253	1.690	.7557
9.	Family Size	–.0056	.2000	.5457
10.	Caste	–1.489	–1.1783	2.0408*
13.	Extension Contact	.1212	.0094	0.2196
14.	Mass Media Exposure	–.0289	–.8085	1.8069
15.	Attitude towards dairy farming	.1212	.2774	0.9375
16.	Economic motivation	.1627	1.0127	1.9430
17.	Value Orientation	.0716	.1552	1.1549
18.	Aspiration	.3126**	.1789	3.8542*
23.	Knowledge	–.0179	–.1335	1.4048

R^2 = 0.3366 F value for R = 3.36*
* = Significant at 0.05 level of probability
** = Significant at 0.01 level of probability

Mahendergarh District

The 13 independent variables were utilized for relational analysis. The results revealed that barring aspiration of the respondents the rest of the variables were found not significantly related with the perception of training needs. Aspiration of the respondents was observed as positively significant at 1 per cent level.

When the same variables were subjected to regression analysis caste was found to have significant negative regression coefficient whereas aspiration was observed to have positive contribution to the dependent variable. All these 13 variables could explain a variation of about 34 per cent and the 'F' value for 'R' was found highly significant.

Later the analysis was conducted by incorporating these variables which had 't' values more than unity. As such land size, family size, extension contact and attitude towards dairying were eliminated from the analysis. Later only 8 variables were utilized in the model and the combined contribution of these variables was upto the time of 28 per cent (Table 4.16).

Table 4.16 : Regression Analysis of Training Needs of Respondents of Mahendergarh District

Sl.No.	of Variable	r	b	t
1.	Age	--.1824	-0.760	.8947
2.	Education	.1055	.9062	1.5978
3.	Family Education	-1.591	-.7003	2.3389*
10.	Caste	-1.489	-.7127	1.7057
16.	Economic Motivation	.1627	.9808	1.9045
17.	Value Orientation	.0716	.1075	0.8059
18.	Aspiration	.3126**	.1782	4.0459**
23.	Knowledge	-.0179	-1.411	1.5685

R^2 = 0.2848 F value for R = 4.53**

* = Significant at 0.05 level of probability

** = Significant at 0.01 level of probability

The results revealed that family education and aspiration came out as the important variables as far as the perception of training needs was concerned. The varibale economic motivation though had high regression coefficient could not come upto the level of significance. The rest five variables failed to demonstrate their contribution to the perception of training needs by rural women.

The variable family education had a significant regression coefficient (b = -0.7003) which indicate that family education was a negative predictor of perception of training nees. It was quite logical to assume that a respondent with high family education might be perceiving lesser needs than another respondent who had low family education score. Family education was found significantly and positively correlated with caste (r=0.3141). Hence, high caste people who were likely to possess high family education score might be involving themselves in dairying to a very little extent and as each their perception of training needs might to a low caste category might be involving more in the dairy farming activities and might be perceiving more training needs (Table 4.16).

Another variable wit notable regression coefficient was aspiration which had a positive contribution. A respondents whose aspirations were more on dairy farming would like to undergo more and more training in order to utilize those skills learnt to reach her goals and as such she perceived more training needs than her counterpart whose aspirations wer comparatively low.

The above findings have been not supported by Pawar (1979), Minhas (1978) and Omprakash (1988) while Fulzele (1986) have supported the above findings.

Kurukshetra District

It was pointed out earlier that the perception of training needs by the respondents of Kurukshetra district was lower than that of Mahendergarh district. However, the relational analysis (Table 4.17) showed that aspiration and economic motivation were found to be

Table 4.17 : Regression Analysis of Training Needs of Respondents of Kurukshetra District

Sl.No.	*of Variable*	*r*	*b*	*t*
1.	Age	–.1422	–.0286	.0581
2.	Education	.0838	–.0488	.2822
3.	Family Education	.0604	.0261	.2081
5.	Land Size	.1196	.0002	.1192
7.	Milk Consumption	.0864	–.0413	.1619
9.	Family Size	–.0742	.0401	.2132
10.	Caste	.1286	–.1454	.3609
13.	Extension Contact	.0494	–.0074	.0475
14.	Mass Media Exposure	.1896	.3358	.7352
15.	Attitude towards dairy farming	.1259	.1425	.2226
16.	Economic motivation	.2309*	.8914	.4636
17.	Value Orientation	.0205	–.1067	.0935
18.	Aspiration	.2399*	.0604	.0424
23.	Knowledge	.1934	.0390	.1035

R^2 = 0.1349 F value for R = 0.95
* = Significant at 0.05 level of probability
** = Significant at 0.01 level of probability

positively correlated with perception of training needs. The rest of the variable were not significantly related to the perception of training needs.

The findings of multiple regression analysis (Table 4.17) indicated that the percentage of variation explained by all these variables was very poor and the 'F' value for R was also not significant. This showed that the contribution of these variables was not to the extent expected.

When the data were processed further to highlight the few important predictors of perceived training needs, it was found that economic motivation was the only contributor to the dependent variable (Table 4.18)

Table 4.18 : Regression Analysis of Training Needs of Respondents of Kurukshetra District

Sl.No. of Variable	*r*	*b*	*t*
15. Attitude Towards Dairy Farming	.1259	.1818	1:0509
16. Economic Motivation	.2309*	.8513	2.0463*
18. Aspiration	.2399*	.0412	1.8181

R^2 = 0.1036 F value for R = 3.70

* = Significant at 0.05 level of probability

The variable economic motivation came out as a positive predictor of the perception of training needs of farm women. The respondents who had high economic motivation score would like to acquire more skills which result in economic returns ultimately, than those who had low economic motivation. Hence, economic motivation of the respondents was found positively contributing to the perception of training needs. The result revealed the economic motivation had positive relationship with perceived training needs while Omprakash (1988) had different findings.

Aspiration was found to be a positive correlate of the perception of training needs. It implied that perception of training needs goes high with increase in the aspirations of the respondents. However, this variable failed to show its contribution to the dependent variable to a significant level.

Pooled Sample

The data were subjected to correlational analysis to ascertain the correlates of training needs. Initially 13 variables were tried after eliminating some of the variables on the basis of high inter-correlations.

The findings presented in Table 4.19 indicated that aspiration was the only variable which was found highly correlated with training needs of farm women. When all the 13 variables were utilized for regression analysis two more variables caste and economic motivation were found to have significant regression coefficients.

Table 4.19 : Regression Analysis of Training Needs of Respondents in Pooled Sample

Sl.No. of Variable	*r*	*b*	*t*
1. Age	–.1824	–.0705	1.3471
2. Education	.1110	.3756	1.3205
3. Family Education	–.0438	–.2698	1.5376
5. Land Size	.0558	.0393	0.3573
9. Family Size	–.0369	.0678	0.3563
10. Caste	–.0371	–.7108*	2.3139
13. Extension Contact	.1404	.0472	1.8144
14. Mass Media Exposure	.0362	-.4604	1.4044
15. Attitude towards dairy farming	.1227	.1974	1.0941
16. Economic motivation	.1339	.7012*	2.0430
17. Value Orientation	.0389	–.0220	0.2771
18. Aspiration	.2624**	.1353**	4.3791
23. Knowledge	.0380	–.0130	1.2557

R^2 = 0.1990 F value for R = 3.56

* = Significant at 0.05 level of probability

** = Significant at 0.01 level of probability

Caste though not found significantly correlated with training needs, was observed to be contributing negatively to the variation in the training needs of the perception of training needs owing to the cultural characteristics in the villages.

The above findings were differed with the findings of Fulzele (1986) and Omprakash (1988).

The economic motivation was found to be a positive contributor to the training needs as evident by the significant regression coefficient (b=0.7012*). This indicated that an unit increase in economic motivation may improve the perception of training needs by 0.70 units. It was quite logical to believe that those respondents who had high economic motivation tend to acquire more and more skills in their occupations in a bid to satisfy their economic desire by putting those skills into practices. Fulzele (1986) was not found agreed with the above findings.

Similarly aspiration was also came out as an important variable in the regression analysis. It had a high and significant correlation as well as regression coefficients.

All these 13 variables could explain a variation of about 20 per cent in the variation of the perception of training needs.

With a view to find out the few important variables from this long list of 13 variables, five variables which had high 't' values were further subjected to regression analysis. Out of these five variables caste, economic motivation and aspiration were again turned out to be very important variables as far as training needs was concerned. The variables family education and extension contact failed to show their contribution to the dependent variable. The multiple R^2 value was 0.150 and the 'F' value for 'R' was found to be significant (Table 4.20).

Table 4.20 : Regression Analysis of Training Needs of Respondents of Pooled Sample

Sl.No.	*of Variable*	*r*	*b*	*t*
3.	Family Education	–.0438	–.0949	.6655
10.	Caste	–.0371	–.7226**	2.9923
13.	Extension Contact	.1404	.0426	1.6930
16.	Economic Motivation	.1339	.7512**	2.2472
18.	Aspiration	.2624	.1282**	4.6278

R^2 = 0.1500 F value for R = 6.84

* = Significant at 0.05 level of probability

5

SUMMARY AND IMPLICATIONS

India with an annual milk production of 641 lac tonnes 1987-88 ranks third in the world. Milk and milk products plays a vital role in country's economy, being the second largest contributor to the gross agricultural produce.

The women in present age are facing the most challenging situation of performing their roles in and outside the home for social and economic development of the Nation. Although, in past the activities of rural women were mostly confined to domestic chores, in the wake of modernization of agriculture they play an important role in adoption of scientific agriculture and Dairy Farming Practices. There are 321 millions female population in the country and majority of them are confined to Rural India. How, these rural women are brought into main stream of dairy development ? and what are their needs in accepting dairy farming practices ? considering this project has been taken with the following objectives :

1. To identify the role of farm women and to assess their role performance in Dairy Farming Practices.
2. To study the differential level of knowledge of farm women regarding breeding, feeding, management health care.
3. To study the perceived training needs of farm women regarding Dairy Farming Practices.
4. To study the relationship of socio-personal psychological variables with role performance and perceived training

needs in relation to Dairy Farming Practices.

The study has been conducted in Haryana State which comprises of 12 districts. The districts of the state have been categorized into progressive and less progressive categories on the basis of following 12 indicators suggested by scientists and field workers. The indicators are :

1. Literacy percentage of rural women.
2. Cattle and buffalo ratio.
3. Number of milch cows/1000 persons.
4. Number of buffaloes/1000 persons.
5. Density of cattle per Sq. Km.
6. Density of buffaloes per Sq. Km.
7. Percentage of crossbred cattle.
8. Per capita availability of milk in Gms/day.
9. Average livestock population per veterinary institution.
10. Percentage of irrigated area.
11. Average yield of wheat.
12. Average yield of paddy.

The districts have been ranked on the basis of their position in terms of selected indicators. The first rank was given to the highest score i.e. 12 and the twelfth rank was assigned to lowest score as one. The total score in terms of 12 indicators were calculated by adding their respective scores. The mean was calculated and on the basis of mean score the districts were categorized as progressive one's having score above mean and less progressive districts having score below mean. The progressive districts in order of rank were Kurukshetra, Sonepat, Karnal, Ambala and Jind and non-progressive districts were Hissar, Sirsa, Rohtak, Gurgaon, Bhiwani, Faridabad and Mahendergarh. The Kurukshetra district was selected as most progressive and Mahendergarh as least progressive district of Haryana in the present study.

The women of Kurukshetra and Mahendergarh district constituted the population of the study. Out of the farm women, such women were selected who own at least one milch cattle and buffalo and devoting more time for caring the animals. There are four categories of women households i.e. Landless, Small, Medium and Large farmers.

There were 8 blocks in Kurukshetra district and 9 in Mahendergarh district, out of these two blocks were selected from each district randomly. Two villages were selected from each of the four blocks on the basis of distance from block headquarters. Thus, there were 8 villages. 25 respondents were selected from each village allocated proportionately to the four categories of women households subjected to minimum number of five from each category by random sampling method. In all there were 200 respondents.

Salient Findings

I. Personal Profile of the Respondents

1. Majority of the farm women (above 60 per cent) in all the settings namely, Mahendergarh, Kurukshetra and in pooled sample were in the middle age group. They were in the age group ranging from 24 to 42 years.

2. Majority of the farm women, 41 per cent in Mahendergarh, 68 per cent in Kurukshetra and 54.5 per cent in pooled sample were illiterate.

3. In Mahendergarh district 14, 72 and 14 per cent respondents had low, medium and high family education level respectively whereas the corresponding figures for Kurukshetra were 17, 60 and 23 per cent respectively. In case of pooled sample the family education level were 17, 66 and 17 per cent respectively.

4. Large number of farm women (about 80 per cent) were rearing animals ranging from 4 to 10 and the mean herd size was 7 animals per family.

5. Seventy per cent of respondents were in medium level of milk production in Mahendergarh district, 73 per cent in Kurukshetra and 68 per cent in pooled sample.

6. More than 50 per cent of the farm women were in medium level of milk consumption category in Mahendergarh, Kurukshetra and in pooled sample.

7. Sixty eight per cent farm women in Mahendergarh district were

in the medium milk sale category whereas majority (64 per cent) in Kurukshetra were in low level of milk sale. In pooled sample 30, 57.5 and 13.5 per cent were in high, medium and low level of milk sale category respectively.

8. The average family size of the pooled sample was found to be about 7 members. These were fewer respondents 14 per cent in low family size category in Kurukshetra compare to 28 per cent in Mahendergarh in the same category.

9. 37 and 32 per cent respondents in Mahendergarh belong to high and low caste group respectively whereas 45 and 35 per cent respondents of Kurukshetra belong to high and low caste group respectively. In pooled sample 29 per cent belong to low caste group.

10. Majority of the farm women had low and medium level of extension contact and mass media exposure in all the settings.

11. About 60 per cent respondents of Mahendergarh and Kurukshetra districts had neutral level of attitude towards dairy farming whereas 16 and 26 per cent respondents had favourable attitude. In pooled sample only 13.5 per cent respondents had favourable attitude towards dairy farming practices.

12. About 71 per cent respondents had medium level of economic motivation in Kurukshetra whereas only 36 per cent respondents had medium level of economic motivation in Mahendergarh district.

13. There were 43 per cent respondents with medium level of value orientation in Mahendergarh district. Respondents in Kurukshetra district had more or less equal distribution among low, medium and high levels of value orientation.

14. In Mahendergarh 69 per cent respondents had medium level of aspiration whereas 59 per cent respondents of Kurukshetra had in the higher category.

II. Role Performance of Farm Women in Relation to Dairy Farming Practices

The role performance in this study was carried out by obtaining responses on 23 specific dairying areas. Majority of the respondents occupied the medium level of role performance.

Mahendergarh district showed the largest majority of the respondents falling in the medium level of role performance with a distribution of about 82, 97, 78 and 65 per cent among landless, small, medium and large farmers, respectively. The corresponding distributions in Kurukshetra and pooled sample were about 68, 59, 83 and 65 per cent and 77, 88, 74 and 68 per cent respectively.

III. Time Spent on Dairy Farming Activities

1. Regarding the time spent on dairy farming practices by the farm women, in Mahendergarh 6.7 hours, in Kurukshetra 4.5 hours and in pooled sample 5.6 hours per day were spent on animals caring activities.

2. On an average each respondent was spending about 4.15 hours per day in Mahendergarh and 2.22 hours per day in Kurukshetra district on feeding of animals.

3. Very less time was spent on activities related animal health care. It was only 0.10 hours per day in Kurukshetra and 0.15 hours per day in Mahendergarh districts.

4. In pooled sample landless farm women devoted maximum time 6.16 hours per day on animals caring activities.

5. On fodder and feeding of the animals landless women were spending 5.25 hours per day in Mahendergarh district as compared to 3.44 hours per day in Kurukshetra district.

6. In the area of fodder and feeding of animals the activities which consumed maximum time of the farm women were fodder harvesting, feeding to animals and watering to animals in both the districts.

7. The respondents were spending about half an hour per day in milking of animals and a little over quarter of an hour in a care and heating of milk in both the districts.

8. Care of newly born calf was an activity on which they were spending about 5 minutes per day in both the areas.

IV. Differential Knowledge Level of Farm Women Regarding Dairy Farming

1. Majority of respondents in all the settings namely Mahendergarh,

Kurukshetra and in pooled sample were in medium level of knowledge about breeding.

2. In Mahendergarh district about 54, 41, 39 and 55 per cent farm women were falling in the medium level of knowledge regarding feeding of animals among the landless, small, medium and large land holdings of farm women respectively. In Kurukshetra district about 82, 59, 58 and 60 per cent respondents had low level of knowledge regarding feeding of animals among landless, small, medium and large land holdings respectively.

3. In all the three settings, majority (30 per cent to 80 per cent) farm women among landless, small, medium and large holding sizes were occupying medium level of knowledge regarding management of animals.

4. Regarding health care in Mahendergarh respondents distribution in accordance with the landless, small, medium and large land holdings were 86, 50, 52 and 35 per cent respectively in low level of knowledge. In Kurukshetra district medium level were about 35, 59, 42 and 85 per cent respectively among landless, small, medium and large farm women.

V. Training Needs

1. In all the three settings majority of the respondents occupied the medium level of training needs.

2. The medium level of training needs was observed among landless, small, medium and large land holding farm women was about 75, 55, 91 and 75 per cent in Mahendergarh, 79, 96, 75 and 85 per cent in Kurukshetra district. In case of Pooled Sample about 69, 65, 87 and 75 per cent were in medium level of training needs in different categories respectively.

3. Among the five areas of dairy farming, farm women were mostly interested in training on health care of dairy animals in all the settings.

4. In all the settings breeding was shown as a second preference for training.

5. Feeding of animals was assigned third rank in Mahendergarh whereas in Kurukshetra it was given fourth rank.

6. Farm women of Kurukshetra district did not want training regarding fodder production. It was ranked sixth and management stood at rank fifth.
7. Fourty nine per cent of farm women preferred 5 days duration for training and only 24 per cent preferred 3 days duration.
8. Majority (50%) opined that training programme should be organised in the month of March.
9. Seventy six per cent farm women want that training programme should be organised either at village or at Block Headquarter.

VI. Relational Analysis of Role Performance

1. In Mahendergarh education, milk sale, time spent on dairy farming and extension contact were positively and significantly related with role performance, whereas age, family size and milk consumption had significant but negative relationship with role performance of farm women.
2. Family educational status, land holding size, milk consumption, caste, extension contact and value orientation had significant but negative relationship with role performance of farm women in Kurukshetra district. Two variables namely, time spent and level of aspiration had significant and positive relationship with role performance.
3. In pooled sample age, land holding size, milk consumption, family size and caste had negative and significant relationship with role performance of farm women, whereas milk sale, time spent, extension contact, mass media exposure and economic motivation were positively and significantly related with role performance.
4. Time spent on dairy farming activities by farm women had very high correlational value with role performance in all the three settings.

VII. Rational Analysis of Training Needs

1. Out of 19 variables only two variables i.e. time spent and level of aspiration had shown positive and significant association with the training needs in Mahendergarh district as their 'r' values were significant at .01% level.

2. In Kurukshetra district economic motivation and level of aspiration had shown positive relationship with training needs.
3. Time spent and level of aspiration had significant and positive relationship with training needs in case of pooled sample.

Implications

The findings of the study will be helpful to planners and administrators for planning the dairy development programmes for farm women.

On the basis of results, training programme of farm women in dairy farming practices can be organised to improve their performance and skill.

Krishi Vigyan Kendra can plan their training programmes as felt needs of the farm women.

Future Suggestions

The study was carried out in two districts of Haryana on their progressiveness. Therefore, such studies may be carried out in other districts of Haryana as well as in other states.

As few variables were correlated with training needs of farm women, more variables may be explore for such studies.

BIBLIOGRAPHY

Anonymous (1989) : National Commission on self employed women (1989) in Singhal, S.; Yadav, L. and Gandhi, S. — A resource in development, *Indian Journal of Adult Education*, 50(2), 59–61.

Bloom, B.S. ; Enoathardt, M.; Furst, S.; Hill, W. and Krathwhol, D.R. (1956) "Taxonomy of Educational Objectives". *The cognitive domine*, Longmans, Green & Co., New York.

Chakravorty, S. (1975) "Women power in Agriculture" *Kurukshetra* 24(4) 8.

Chauhan, K.N.K. (1976) "Inducing change through site study of some socio-psychological and communication correlates of adoption behaviour of the rural audience of site in North Bihar" Unpublished Ph.D. Thesis.

Davis Kingsley (1948) "The human society", the Mac Millan Co. New York.

Devi, A.L. and Reddy, S.V. (1984) "Role expectations of rural women in farm activities" *Indian Jr. of Extn. Edu.* 20(3–4) 27–34.

Downie, N.M. and Heath, R.W. (1965) "Basic Statistical Methods" Harper K. Row Publishers, New York.

Dubey, V.K.; Singh, Sukhbir and Khera, J.K (1978) "Role of rural women in farm decision making" *Annual Report*, NDRI, p. 244.

English, H.B. and English, A.C. (1958) "A comprehensive dictionary of psychological and psychological terms" Longmans, Green & Co., New York.

Flippo, E.R. (1966) "Principles of personal mangement". Tokyo Kogakhusha Company Ltd.

Frank, J.D. (1935) "Individual differences in certain aspects of level of aspiration". *American J. of Psychology*, XL–VII pp. 119–128.

Fulzele, R.M. (1986) "Multi dimensional analysis of training programme of KVK. Ph.D. thesis, unpublished, Kurukshetra University, Kurukshetra.

FAO (1986) "*FAO Production Year Book*" Vol. 40, pp. 199.

Gill, H.S. (1970) "Training needs of farmers for high yielding varieties programme in Ludhiana district–Punjab. M.Sc. Thesis, PAU, Ludhiana.

Gill, S.S. and Minhas, P.S. (1978) "Training needs of dairy farmers". *Ind. Dairyman*, Vol. XXX (6), 431–34.

Gite, N.R. (1980) "A study on training needs of landless crossbred cattle owners under 'Lab to land 'programme". M.Sc. Thesis (unpublished), Kurukshetra University, Kurukshetra.

Guilford, J.P. and Fruchter, B. (1978) "Fundamental statistics in Psychology and Education" 6th Edition, Mc Graw Hill Kogakusha Ltd. Tokyo.

Gupta, C.L. (1976) "A study of differential motives of dairy farmers of milk cooperative society of ICDP Karnal towards dairy innovations". Unpublished Ph.D. Thesis, Punjab Univ. Chandigarh.

Gupta, D.D. and Singh, .V.K. (1986) "Participation of women in different farm and non form activities in Haryana" Report presented in Seminar as role of development programme on Socio-economic status of women. Deptt. of Agril. Economics, HAU, Hissar.

Haque, A. (1968) "A study of need interest ant leisure time activities of school going rural girl" M.Sc. Thesis, IARI unpublished, New Delhi.

Jain, D. (1980) "Milk producers of Kaira women quest for power"

Vikash Publishing House, New Delhi.

Jately, S. (1981) "*Impact of planned social change of rural women*" ICSSR Research Abstract 10(1–2) 1–16.

Kadian, Kehar Singh (1988) "A study of differential motives of farm women with respect to dairy farming of ICDP Karnal (Haryana)". M.Sc. thesis (Unpublished), Kurukshetra University, Kurukshetra.

Kaur, Jaswant (1981) "A study of differential dairying knowledge and role performance of trained and untrained milk producers and their wives". M.Sc. thesis (unpublished), Kurukshetra University, Kurukshetra.

Kaur, Satnam (1986) "Role of rural development in Haryana"—A case study. Ph.D. Thesis, HAU, Hissar, unpublished.

Kokate, K.D. (1980) "A study on training needs as perceived by the farmers of K.V.K. villages Karnal". M.Sc. thesis (unpublished), Kurukshetra University, Kurukshetra.

*Krech, Davis and Crutchfield, R.S. (1948) "Role performance and role prediction" Ph.D. Thesis of Kherde, R.L., IARI, New Delhi.

Kumar, K. and Mage, S.L. (1974) "Training needs of farm women in Haryana". *Indian J. Adult Edu.* 35(10) 72–73.

Leagnes, J.P. (1961) "Programme planning to meet people's needs" Ministry of Food and Agri. Govt. of India".

Lindquist, H.F. (1951) "Educational measurement, Washington, D.C. American Council of Education".

Linton, Ralph (1945) "The cultural background of personality" D. Appletion century crots, Inc. New York.

Lynton, R.P. and Pareek, U. (1967) "Training for development" Illinois Richard, D. Irvin Inc.

Mulay, S. and Ray, G.L. (1973) "Towards modernization : A study of rural peasantry in rural Delhi" National Publishing House, Delhi.

Omprakash (1988) "A study of training needs of farm women in scientific dairy farming practices in Karnal district of Haryana". M.Sc. thesis, unpublished, Kurukshetra University, Kurukshetra.

Patil, K.F. and Kale, J.V. (1972) "Vocational Training needs of farmers with a special reference to the contents and types of training. *Ind. Jr. Extn. Edu.* 7(3 & 4) : 14–21.

Pawar, S.G. (1979) "A study of training needs of members of primary milk producers society in Satara district (Maharashtra)" M.Sc. Thesis, Unpublished, Kurukshetra University, Kurukshetra.

Puri, S. (1974) "Role of farm women in animal husbandry programme" Kurukshetra 22 (23) :9.

Ram Chand (1980) "Measurement of aspiration of dairy farmers of ICDP Karnal with projective and non-projective technique" Ph.D Thesis (unpublished), Kurukshetra University, Kurukshetra.

Rizvi, R.S. (1967) "Job analysis, Job performance and suitability of pre-service". Training of Gram Savikas in three selected states. M.Sc. Thesis (unpublished), IARI, New Delhi.

Rogers, E.M. and Shoemaker, F.F. (1971) "Communication of innovations". The Free Press, New York.

Sargent, Stansferd (1951) "Concept of role and ego in contemporary psychology social psychology at crossbred, in Rohner and Sherif" Harper & Brothers, New York.

Saroj (Mrs.), Kashyap (1988) "Human resource development with special reference to time use analysis and feasibility of vocational trainings".

Sharma, A. (1974) "Information needs of farm women regarding selected agricultural and home science practices" M.Sc. thesis, PAU, Ludhiana.

Sharma, KNS; Aggarwal, S.B. and Sunderesan, D. (1980) "Report on the survey of study bovine development and milk production in Key Village and non-key village area of Karnal district".

Singh, A.P. (1967) "Some issues in training of extension personnel," *Ind. J. Soc. Work*, 18(3) : 317.

Singh, Khajan (1982) "A study of aspiration of farm women in Karnal district" M.Sc. Thesis (unpublished), NDRI, Karnal.

Singh, K.N. and Singh, S.N. (1976) "Effective communication media for rural audiences. An experimental study". The Dharmri

Morarji Chemical Co. Ltd., Erospect Chamber, Bombay.

Singh, Nilini (1979) "Cited in Brita. B. 1979 *Op. cit.*

Singh, T.R. (1968) "An analysis of rationality in decision making in relation to the adoption of innovation of varying nature" Unpublished, Ph.D. Thesis, IARI, New Delhi.

Snedecor, G.W. and Cochran, W.G. (1967) "Statistical methods" Oxford and IBH Pub. Co., New Delhi.

Thurstone, L.L. (1946) "The measurement of aptitude", *American Jr. of Sociology*, Chicago Uni. Press, Chicago, 52.

Trivedi, G. (1963) "Measurement and analysis of socio-economic status of rural families" Ph.D. theis (unpublished), IARI, New Delhi.

Verma, O.S. and Malik, B.S. (1984) "Contribution of Farm ladies in farm operations". *Jr. of Home Science*, Vol. 15 : 2 : pp. 57–59.

INDEX